THE SORROWS OF YOUNG WERTHER

JOHAAN WOLFGANG VON GOETHE

Translated by R.D. Boylan

Edited by Nathen Haskell Dole

SANAGE
PUBLISHING HOUSE

Paperback: 978-811987535-1
Hardback: 978-811987563-4
eBook: 978-811987518-4

Printed by:

Sanage Publishing House LLP
Mumbai, India

sanagepublishing@gmail.com

Johann Wolfgang (von) Goethe[a] (28 August 1749 – 22 March 1832) is widely regarded as the greatest and most influential writer in the German language. His work has had a profound and wide-ranging influence on Western literary, political, and philosophical thought from the late 18th century to the present day.

Goethe composed The Sorrows of Young Werther in 1774. Goethe accepted an invitation from the Duke of Weimar in 1775 to join his court and for a decade held various official positions there. He spent 1787 in Italy, where he wrote Iphigenie auf Tauris and worked on the first part of Faust (1808). In 1791, Goethe was appointed director of the ducal theater, a position he held for twenty-two years. In 1806, Goethe married Christiane Vulpius, the mother of his four children. In the last year of his life, Goethe completed the second part of his masterpiece, Faust.

The American philosopher and essayist Ralph Waldo Emerson selected Goethe as one of six "representative men" in his work of the same name (along with Plato, Emanuel Swedenborg, Montaigne, Napoleon, and Shakespeare).

CONTENTS

PREFACE

I have carefully collected whatever I have been able to learn of the story of poor Werther, and here present it to you, knowing that you will thank me for it. To his spirit and character, you cannot refuse your admiration and love: to his fate you will not deny your tears.

And thou, good soul, who sufferest the same distress as he endured once, draw comfort from his sorrows; and let this little book be thy friend, if, owing to fortune or through thine own fault, thou canst not find a dearer companion.

BOOK I

MAY 4.

How happy I am that I am gone! My dear friend, what a thing is the heart of man! To leave you, from whom I have been inseparable, whom I love so dearly, and yet to feel happy! I know you will forgive me. Have no other attachments been specially appointed by fate to torment a head like mine? Poor Leonora! and yet I was not to blame. Was it my fault, that, whilst the peculiar charms of her sister afforded me an agreeable entertainment, a passion for me was engendered in her feeble heart? And yet am I wholly blameless? Did I not encourage her emotions? Did I not feel charmed at those truly genuine expressions of nature, which, though but little mirthful in reality, so often amused us? Did I not—but oh! what is man, that he dares so to accuse himself? My dear friend I promise you I will improve; I will no longer, as has ever been my habit, continue to ruminate on every petty vexation which fortune may dispense; I will enjoy the present, and the past shall be for me the past. No doubt you are right, my best of friends, there would be far less suffering amongst mankind, if men—and God knows why they are so fashioned—did not employ their imaginations so assiduously in recalling the memory of past sorrow, instead of bearing their present lot with equanimity. Be kind enough to inform my mother that I shall attend to her business to the best of my ability and shall give her the earliest information about it.

I have seen my aunt and find that she is very far from being the disagreeable person our friends allege her to be. She is a lively, cheerful woman, with the best of hearts. I explained to her my mother's wrongs with regard to that part of her portion which has been withheld from her. She told me the motives and reasons of her own conduct, and the terms on which she is willing to give up the whole, and to do more than we have asked. In short, I cannot write further upon this subject at present; only assure my mother that all will go on well. And I have again observed, my dear friend, in this trifling affair, that misunderstandings and neglect occasion more mischief in the world than even malice and wickedness. At all events, the two latter are of less frequent occurrence.

In other respects, I am very well off here. Solitude in this terrestrial paradise is a genial balm to my mind, and the young spring cheers with its bounteous promises my oftentimes misgiving heart. Every tree, every bush, is full of flowers; and one might wish himself transformed into a butterfly, to float about in this ocean of perfume, and find his whole existence in it.

The town itself is disagreeable; but then, all around, you find an inexpressible beauty of nature. This induced the late Count M to lay out a garden on one of the sloping hills which here intersect each other with the most charming variety and form the loveliest valleys. The garden is simple; and it is easy to perceive, even upon your first entrance, that the plan was not designed by a scientific gardener, but by a man who wished to give himself up here to the enjoyment of his own sensitive heart. Many a tear have I already shed to the memory of its departed master in a summerhouse which is now reduced to ruins, but was his favourite resort, and now is mine. I shall soon be master of the place. The gardener has become attached to me within the last few days, and he will lose nothing thereby.

MAY 10.

A wonderful serenity has taken possession of my entire soul, like these sweet mornings of spring which I enjoy with my whole heart. I am alone, and feel the charm of existence in this spot, which was created for the bliss of souls like mine. I am so happy, my dear friend, so absorbed in the exquisite sense of mere tranquil existence, that I neglect my talents. I should be incapable of drawing a single stroke at the present moment; and yet I feel that I never was a greater artist than now. When, while the lovely valley teems with vapour around me, and the meridian sun strikes the upper surface of the impenetrable foliage of my trees and but a few stray gleams steal into the inner sanctuary, I throw myself down among the tall grass by the trickling stream; and, as I lie close to the earth, a thousand unknown plants are noticed by me: when I hear the buzz of the little world among the stalks, and grow familiar with the countless indescribable forms of the insects and flies, then I feel the presence of the Almighty, who formed us in his own image, and the breath of that universal love which bears and sustains us, as it floats around us in an eternity of bliss; and then, my friend, when darkness overspreads my eyes, and heaven and earth seem to dwell in my soul and absorb its power, like the form of a beloved mistress, then I often think with longing, Oh, would I could describe these conceptions, could impress upon paper all that is living so full and warm within me, that it might be the mirror of my soul, as my soul is the mirror of the infinite God! O my friend—but it is too much for my strength—I sink under the weight of the splendour of these visions!

MAY 12.

I know not whether some deceitful spirits haunt this spot, or whether it be the warm, celestial fancy in my own heart which makes everything around me seem like paradise. In front of the house is a fountain, —a fountain to which I am bound by a charm like Melusina and her sisters. Descending a gentle slope, you come to an arch, where, some twenty steps lower down, water of the clearest crystal gushes from the marble rock. The narrow wall which encloses it above, the tall trees which encircle the spot, and the coolness of the place itself, —everything imparts a pleasant but sublime impression. Not a day passes on which I do not spend an hour there. The young maidens come from the town to fetch water, —innocent and necessary employment, and formerly the occupation of the daughters of kings. As I take my rest there, the idea of the old patriarchal life is awakened around me. I see them, our old ancestors, how they formed their friendships and contracted alliances at the fountain-side; and I feel how fountains and streams were guarded by beneficent spirits. He who is a stranger to these sensations has never really enjoyed cool repose at the side of a fountain after the fatigue of a weary summer day.

MAY 13.

You ask if you shall send me books. My dear friend, I beseech you, for the love of God, relieve me from such a yoke! I need no more to be guided, agitated, heated. My heart ferments sufficiently of itself. I want strains to lull me, and I find them to perfection in my Homer. Often do I strive to allay the burning fever of my blood; and you have never witnessed anything so unsteady, so uncertain, as my heart. But need I confess this to you, my dear friend, who have so often endured the anguish of witnessing my sudden transitions from sorrow to immoderate joy, and from sweet melancholy to violent passions? I treat my poor heart like a sick child and gratify its every fancy. Do not mention this again: there are people who would censure me for it.

MAY 15.

The common people of the place know me already, and love me, particularly the children. When at first, I associated with them, and inquired in a friendly tone about their various trifles, some fancied that I wished to ridicule them, and turned from me in exceeding ill-humour. I did not allow that circumstance to grieve me: I only felt most keenly what I have often before observed. Persons who can claim a certain rank keep themselves coldly aloof from the common people, as though they feared to lose their importance by the contact; whilst wanton idlers, and such as are prone to bad joking, affect to descend to their level, only to make the poor people feel their impertinence all the more keenly.

I know very well that we are not all equal, nor can be so; but it is my opinion that he who avoids the common people, in order not to lose their respect, is as much to blame as a coward who hides himself from his enemy because he fears defeat.

The other day I went to the fountain, and found a young servant-girl, who had set her pitcher on the lowest step, and looked around to see if one of her companions was approaching to place it on her head. I ran down and looked at her. "Shall I help you, pretty lass?" said I. She blushed deeply. "Oh, sir!" she exclaimed. "No ceremony!" I replied. She adjusted her headgear, and I helped her. She thanked me and ascended the steps.

MAY 17.

I have made all sorts of acquaintances but have as yet found no society. I know not what attraction I possess for the people, so many of them like me, and attach themselves to me; and then I feel sorry when the road we pursue together goes only a short distance.

If you inquire what the people are like here, I must answer, "The same as everywhere." The human race is but a monotonous affair. Most of them labour the greater part of their time for mere subsistence; and the scanty portion of freedom which remains to them so troubles them that they use every exertion to get rid of it. Oh, the destiny of man!

But they are a right good sort of people. If I occasionally forget myself, and take part in the innocent pleasures which are not yet forbidden to the peasantry, and enjoy myself, for instance, with genuine freedom and sincerity, round a well-covered table, or arrange an excursion or a dance opportunely, and so forth, all this produces a good effect upon my disposition; only I must forget that there lie dormant within me so many other qualities which moulder uselessly, and which I am obliged to keep carefully concealed. Ah! this thought affects my spirits fearfully. And yet to be misunderstood is the fate of the like of us.

Alas, that the friend of my youth is gone! Alas, that I ever knew her! I might say to myself, "You are a dreamer to seek what is not to be found here below." But she has been mine. I have possessed that heart, that noble soul, in whose presence I seemed to be more than I really was, because I was all that I could be. Good heavens! did then a single power of my soul remain unexercised? In her presence could I not display, to its full extent, that mysterious feeling with which my heart embraces nature? Was not our intercourse a perpetual web of the finest emotions, of the keenest wit, the varieties of which, even in their very eccentricity, bore the stamp of genius? Alas! the few years by which she was my senior brought her to the grave before me. Never can I forget her firm mind or her heavenly patience.

A few days ago, I met a certain young V—, a frank, open fellow, with a most pleasing countenance. He has just left the university, does not deem himself overwise, but believes he knows more than other people. He has worked hard, as I can perceive from many circumstances, and, in short, possesses a large stock of information. When he heard that I am drawing a good deal, and that I know Greek (two wonderful things for this part of the country), he came to see me, and displayed his whole store of learning, from Batteaux to Wood, from De Piles to Winkelmann: he assured me he had read through the first part of Sultzer's theory, and also possessed a manuscript of Heyne's work on the study of the antique. I allowed it all to pass.

I have become acquainted, also, with a very worthy person, the district judge, a frank and open-hearted man. I am told it is a most delightful thing to see him in the midst of his children, of whom he has nine. His eldest daughter especially is highly spoken of. He has invited me to go and see him, and I intend to do so on the first opportunity. He lives at one of the royal hunting-lodges, which can be reached from here in an hour and a half by walking, and which he obtained leave to inhabit after the loss of his wife, as it is so painful to him to reside in town and at the court.

There have also come in my way a few other originals of a questionable sort, who are in all respects undesirable, and most intolerable in their demonstration of friendship. Good-bye. This letter will please you: it is quite historical.

MAY 22.

That the life of man is but a dream, many a man has surmised heretofore; and I, too, am everywhere pursued by this feeling. When I consider the narrow limits within which our active and inquiring faculties are confined; when I see how all our energies are wasted in providing for mere necessities, which again have no further end than to prolong a wretched existence; and then that all our satisfaction concerning certain subjects of investigation ends in nothing better than a passive resignation, whilst we amuse ourselves painting our prison-walls with bright figures and brilliant landscapes,—when I consider all this, Wilhelm, I am silent. I examine my own being, and find there a world, but a world rather of imagination and dim desires, than of distinctness and living power. Then everything swims before my senses, and I smile and dream while pursuing my way through the world.

All learned professors and doctors are agreed that children do not comprehend the cause of their desires; but that the grown-up should wander about this earth like children, without knowing whence they come, or whither they go, influenced as little by fixed motives, but guided like them by biscuits, sugar-plums, and the rod,—this is what nobody is willing to acknowledge; and yet I think it is palpable.

I know what you will say in reply; for I am ready to admit that they are happiest, who, like children, amuse themselves with their playthings, dress and undress their dolls, and attentively watch the cupboard, where mamma has locked up her sweet things, and, when at last they get a delicious morsel, eat it greedily, and exclaim, "More!" These are certainly happy beings; but others also are objects of envy, who dignify their paltry employments, and sometimes even their passions, with pompous titles, representing them to mankind as gigantic achievements performed for their welfare and glory. But the man who humbly acknowledges the vanity of all this, who observes with what pleasure the thriving citizen converts his little garden into a paradise, and how patiently even the poor man pursues his weary way under his burden, and how all wish equally to behold the light of the sun a little longer,—yes, such a man is at peace, and creates his own world within himself; and he is also happy, because he is a man. And then, however limited his sphere, he still preserves in his bosom the sweet feeling of liberty and knows that he can quit his prison whenever he likes.

MAY 26.

You know of old my ways of settling anywhere, of selecting a little cottage in some cosy spot, and of putting up in it with every inconvenience. Here, too, I have discovered such a snug, comfortable place, which possesses peculiar charms for me.

About a league from the town is a place called Walheim. (The reader need not take the trouble to look for the place thus designated. We have found it necessary to change the names given in the original.) It is delightfully situated on the side of a hill; and, by proceeding along one of the footpaths which lead out of the village, you can have a view of the whole valley. A good old woman lives there, who keeps a small inn. She sells wine, beer, and coffee, and is cheerful and pleasant notwithstanding her age. The chief charm of this spot consists in two linden-trees, spreading their enormous branches over the little green before the church, which is entirely surrounded by peasants' cottages, barns, and homesteads. I have seldom seen a place so retired and peaceable; and there often have my table and chair brought out from the little inn, and drink my coffee there, and read my Homer. Accident brought me to the spot one fine afternoon, and I found it perfectly deserted. Everybody was in the fields except a little boy about four years of age, who was sitting on the ground, and held between his knees a child about six months old: he pressed it to his bosom with both arms, which thus formed a sort of armchair; and, notwithstanding the liveliness which sparkled in its black eyes, it remained perfectly still. The sight charmed me. I sat down upon a plough opposite and sketched with great delight this little picture of brotherly tenderness. I added the neighbouring hedge, the barn-door, and some broken cartwheels, just as they happened to lie; and I found in about an hour that I had made a very correct and interesting drawing, without putting in the slightest thing of my own. This confirmed me in my resolution of adhering, for the future, entirely to nature. She alone is inexhaustible, and capable of forming the greatest masters. Much may be alleged in favour of rules, as much may be likewise advanced in favour of the laws of society: an artist formed upon them will never produce anything absolutely bad or disgusting; as a man who observes the laws, and obeys decorum, can never be an absolutely intolerable neighbour, nor a decided villain: but yet, say what you will of rules, they destroy the genuine feeling of nature, as well as its true expression. Do not tell me "That this is too hard, that they only restrain and prune superfluous branches, etc." My good friend, I will illustrate this by an analogy. These things resemble love. A warmhearted youth becomes strongly attached to a maiden:

he spends every hour of the day in her company, wears out his health, and lavishes his fortune, to afford continual proof that he is wholly devoted to her. Then comes a man of the world, a man of place and respectability, and addresses him thus: "My good young friend, love is natural; but you must love within bounds. Divide your time: devote a portion to business and give the hours of recreation to your mistress. Calculate your fortune; and out of the superfluity you may make her a present, only not too often, —on her birthday, and such occasions." Pursuing this advice, he may become a useful member of society, and I should advise every prince to give him an appointment; but it is all up with his love, and with his genius if he be an artist. O my friend! why is it that the torrent of genius so seldom bursts forth, so seldom rolls in full-flowing stream, overwhelming your astounded soul? Because, on either side of this stream, cold and respectable persons have taken up their abodes, and, forsooth, their summerhouses and tulip-beds would suffer from the torrent; wherefore they dig trenches, and raise embankments betimes, in order to avert the impending danger.

MAY 27.

I find I have fallen into raptures, declamation, and similes, and have forgotten, in consequence, to tell you what became of the children. Absorbed in my artistic contemplations, which I briefly described in my letter of yesterday, I continued sitting on the plough for two hours. Toward evening a young woman, with a basket on her arm, came running toward the children, who had not moved all that time. She exclaimed from a distance, "You are a good boy, Philip!" She gave me greeting, I returned it, rose, and approached her. I inquired if she were the mother of those pretty children. "Yes," she said; and, giving the eldest a piece of bread, she took the little one in her arms and kissed it with a mother's tenderness. "I left my child in Philip's care," she said, "whilst I went into the town with my eldest boy to buy some wheaten bread, some sugar, and an earthen pot." I saw the various articles in the basket, from which the cover had fallen. "I shall make some broth to-night for my little Hans (which was the name of the youngest): that wild fellow, the big one, broke my pot yesterday, whilst he was scrambling with Philip for what remained of the contents." I inquired for the eldest; and she had scarcely time to tell me that he was driving a couple of geese home from the meadow, when he ran up, and handed Philip an osier-twig. I talked a little longer with the woman and found that she was the daughter of the schoolmaster, and that her husband was gone on a journey into Switzerland for some money a relation had left him. "They wanted to cheat him," she said, "and would not answer his letters; so, he is gone there himself. I hope he has met with no accident, as I have heard nothing of him since his departure." I left the woman, with regret, giving each of the children a kreutzer, with an additional one for the youngest, to buy some wheaten bread for his broth when she went to town next; and so, we parted. I assure you, my dear friend, when my thoughts are all in tumult, the sight of such a creature as this tranquilizes my disturbed mind. She moves in a happy thoughtlessness within the confined circle of her existence; she supplies her wants from day to day; and, when she sees the leaves fall, they raise no other idea in her mind than that winter is approaching. Since that time, I have gone out there frequently. The children have become quite familiar with me; and each gets a lump of sugar when I drink my coffee, and they share my milk and bread and butter in the evening. They always receive their kreutzer on Sundays, for the good woman has orders to give it to them when I do not go there after evening service. They are quite at home with me, tell me everything; and I am particularly amused with observing their tempers, and the simplicity of their behaviour, when some of the other village children are assembled with them.

It has given me a deal of trouble to satisfy the anxiety of the mother, lest (as she says) "they should inconvenience the gentleman."

MAY 30.

What I have lately said of painting is equally true with respect to poetry. It is only necessary for us to know what is really excellent, and venture to give it expression; and that is saying much in few words. Today I have had a scene, which, if literally related, would, make the most beautiful idyl in the world. But why should I talk of poetry and scenes and idyls? Can we never take pleasure in nature without having recourse to art?

If you expect anything grand or magnificent from this introduction, you will be sadly mistaken. It relates merely to a peasant-lad, who has excited in me the warmest interest. As usual, I shall tell my story badly; and you, as usual, will think me extravagant. It is Walheim once more—always Walheim—which produces these wonderful phenomena.

A party had assembled outside the house under the linden-trees, to drink coffee. The company did not exactly please me; and, under one pretext or another, I lingered behind.

A peasant came from an adjoining house and set to work arranging some part of the same plough which I had lately sketched. His appearance pleased me; and I spoke to him, inquired about his circumstances, made his acquaintance and as is my wont with persons of that class, was soon admitted into his confidence. He said he was in the service of a young widow, who set great store by him. He spoke so much of his mistress, and praised her so extravagantly, that I could soon see he was desperately in love with her. "She is no longer young," he said: "and she was treated so badly by her former husband that she does not mean to marry again." From his account it was so evident what incomparable charms she possessed for him, and how ardently he wished she would select him to extinguish the recollection of her first husband's misconduct, that I should have to repeat his own words in order to describe the depth of the poor fellow's attachment, truth, and devotion. It would, in fact, require the gifts of a great poet to convey the expression of his features, the harmony of his voice, and the heavenly fire of his eye. No words can portray the tenderness of his every movement and of every feature: no effort of mine could do justice to the scene. His alarm lest I should misconceive his position with regard to his mistress, or question the propriety of her conduct, touched me particularly. The charming manner with which he described her form and person, which, without possessing the graces of youth, won and attached him to her, is inexpressible, and must be left to the imagination. I have never in my life witnessed or fancied or conceived the possibility of such intense devotion, such ardent affections, united with so much purity. Do not blame me if I say that the recollection of this innocence and truth is deeply impressed upon my very soul; that this picture of fidelity and tenderness haunts me everywhere; and that my own heart, as though enkindled by the flame, glows, and burns within me.

I mean now to try and see her as soon as I can: or perhaps, on second thoughts, I had better not; it is better I should behold her through the eyes of her lover. To my sight, perhaps, she would not appear as she now stands before me; and why should I destroy so sweet a picture?

JUNE 16.

"Why do I not write to you?" You lay claim to learning and ask such a question. You should have guessed that I am well—that is to say—in a word, I have made an acquaintance who has won my heart: I have—I know not.

To give you a regular account of the manner in which I have become acquainted with the most amiable of women would be a difficult task. I am a happy and contented mortal, but a poor historian.

An angel! Nonsense! Everybody so describes his mistress; and yet

I find it impossible to tell you how perfect she is, or why she is so perfect: suffice it to say she has captivated all my senses.

So much simplicity with so much understanding—so mild, and yet so resolute—a mind so placid, and a life so active.

But all this is ugly balderdash, which expresses not a single character nor feature. Some other time—but no, not some other time, now, this very instant, will I tell you all about it. Now or never. Well, between ourselves, since I commenced my letter, I have been three times on the point of throwing down my pen, of ordering my horse, and riding out. And yet I vowed this morning that I would not ride today, and yet every moment I am rushing to the window to see how high the sun is.

I could not restrain myself—go to her I must. I have just returned, Wilhelm; and whilst I am taking supper, I will write to you. What a delight it was for my soul to see her in the midst of her dear, beautiful children, —eight brothers and sisters!

But, if I proceed thus, you will be no wiser at the end of my letter than you were at the beginning. Attend, then, and I will compel myself to give you the details.

I mentioned to you the other day that I had become acquainted with S—, the district judge, and that he had invited me to go and visit him in his retirement, or rather in his little kingdom. But I neglected going, and perhaps should never have gone, if chance had not discovered to me the treasure which lay concealed in that retired spot. Some of our young people had proposed giving a ball in the country, at which I consented to be present. I offered my hand for the evening to a pretty and agreeable, but rather commonplace, sort of girl from the immediate neighbourhood; and it was agreed that I should engage a carriage, and call upon Charlotte, with my partner and her aunt, to convey them to the ball. My companion informed me, as we drove along through the park to the hunting-lodge, that I should make the acquaintance of a very charming young lady. "Take care," added the aunt, "that you do not lose your heart." "Why?" said I. "Because she is already engaged to a very worthy man," she replied, "who is gone to settle his affairs upon the death of his father and will succeed to a very considerable inheritance." This information possessed no interest for me. When we arrived at the gate, the sun was setting behind the tops of the mountains. The atmosphere was heavy; and the ladies expressed their fears of an approaching storm, as masses of low black clouds were gathering in the horizon. I relieved their anxieties by pretending to be weather-wise, although I myself had some apprehensions lest our pleasure should be interrupted.

I alighted; and a maid came to the door and requested us to wait a moment for her mistress. I walked across the court to a well-built house and ascending the flight of steps in front, opened the door, and saw before me the most charming spectacle I had ever witnessed. Six children, from eleven to two years old, were running about the hall, and surrounding a lady of middle height, with a lovely figure, dressed in a robe of simple white, trimmed with pink ribbons. She was holding a rye loaf in her hand and was cutting slices for the little ones all around, in proportion to their age and appetite. She performed her task in a graceful and affectionate manner; each claimant awaiting his turn with outstretched hands, and boisterously shouting his thanks. Some of them ran away at once, to enjoy their evening meal; whilst others, of a gentler disposition, retired to the courtyard to see the strangers, and to survey the carriage in which their Charlotte was to drive away. "Pray forgive me for giving you the trouble to come for me, and for keeping the ladies waiting: but dressing, and arranging some household duties before I leave, had made me forget my children's supper; and they do not like to take it from anyone but me." I uttered some indifferent compliment: but my whole soul was absorbed by her air, her voice, her manner; and I had scarcely recovered myself when she ran into her room to fetch her gloves and fan. The young ones threw inquiring glances at me from a distance; whilst I approached the youngest, a most delicious little creature. He drew back; and Charlotte, entering at the very moment, said, "Louis, shake hands with your cousin." The little fellow obeyed willingly; and I could not resist giving him a hearty kiss, notwithstanding his rather dirty face. "Cousin," said I to Charlotte, as I handed her down, "do you think I deserve the happiness of being related to you?" She replied, with a ready smile, "Oh! I have such a number of cousins, that I should be sorry if you were the most undeserving of them." In taking leave, she desired her next sister, Sophy, a girl about eleven years old, to take great care of the children, and to say good-bye to papa for her when he came home from his ride. She enjoined to the little ones to obey their sister Sophy as they would herself, upon which some promised that they would; but a little fair-haired girl, about six years old, looked discontented, and said, "But Sophy is not you, Charlotte; and we like you best." The two eldest boys had clambered up the carriage; and, at my request, she permitted them to accompany us a little way through the forest, upon their promising to sit very still, and hold fast.

We were hardly seated, and the ladies had scarcely exchanged compliments, making the usual remarks upon each other's dress, and upon the company they expected to meet, when Charlotte stopped the carriage, and made her brothers get down. They insisted upon kissing her hands once more which the eldest did with all the tenderness of a youth of fifteen, but the other in a lighter and more careless manner. She desired them again to give her love to the children, and we drove off.

The aunt inquired of Charlotte whether she had finished the book she had last sent her. "No," said Charlotte; "I did not like it: you can have it again. And the one before was not much better." I was surprised, upon asking the title, to hear that it was _____. (We feel obliged to suppress the passage in the letter, to prevent anyone from feeling aggrieved; although no author need pay much attention to the opinion of a mere girl, or that of an unsteady young man.)

I found penetration and character in everything she said: every expression seemed to brighten her features with new charms, —with new rays of genius, —which unfolded by degrees, as she felt herself understood.

"When I was younger," she observed, "I loved nothing so much as romances. Nothing could equal my delight when, on some holiday, I could settle down quietly in a corner, and enter with my whole heart and soul into the joys or sorrows of some fictitious Leonora. I do not deny that they even possess some charms for me yet. But I read so seldom, that I prefer books suited exactly to my taste. And I like those authors best whose scenes describe my own situation in life, —and the friends who are about me, whose stories touch me with interest, from resembling my own homely existence, —which, without being absolutely paradise, is, on the whole, a source of indescribable happiness."

I endeavoured to conceal the emotion which these words occasioned, but it was of slight avail; for, when she had expressed so truly her opinion of "The Vicar of Wakefield," and of other works, the names of which I omit (Though the names are omitted, yet the authors mentioned deserve Charlotte's approbation, and will feel it in their hearts when they read this passage. It concerns no other person.), I could no longer contain myself, but gave full utterance to what I thought of it: and it was not until Charlotte had addressed herself to the two other ladies, that I remembered their presence, and observed them sitting mute with astonishment. The aunt looked at me several times with an air of raillery, which, however, I did not at all mind.

We talked of the pleasures of dancing. "If it is a fault to love it," said Charlotte, "I am ready to confess that I prize it above all other amusements. If anything disturbs me, I go to the piano, play an air to which I have danced, and all goes right again directly."

You, who know me, can fancy how steadfastly I gazed upon her rich dark eyes during these remarks, how my very soul gloated over her warm lips and fresh, glowing cheeks, how I became quite lost in the delightful meaning of her words, so much so, that I scarcely heard the actual expressions. In short, I alighted from the carriage like a person in a dream and was so lost to the dim world around me, that I scarcely heard the music which resounded from the illuminated ballroom.

The two Messrs. Andran and a certain N. N. (I cannot trouble myself with the names), who were the aunt's and Charlotte's partners, received us at the carriage-door, and took possession of their ladies, whilst I followed with mine.

We commenced with a minuet. I led out one lady after another, and precisely those who were the most disagreeable could not bring themselves to leave off. Charlotte and her partner began an English country dance, and you must imagine my delight when it was their turn to dance the figure with us. You should see Charlotte dance. She dances with her whole heart and soul: her figure is all harmony, elegance, and grace, as if she were conscious of nothing else, and had no other thought or feeling; and, doubtless, for the moment, every other sensation is extinct.

She was engaged for the second country dance, but promised me the third, and assured me, with the most agreeable freedom, that she was very fond of waltzing. "It is the custom here," she said, "for the previous partners to waltz together; but my partner is an indifferent waltzer and will feel delighted if I save him the trouble. Your partner is not allowed to waltz, and, indeed, is equally incapable but I observed during the country dance that you waltz well; so, if you will waltz with me, I beg you would propose it to my partner, and I will propose it to yours." We agreed, and it was arranged that our partners should mutually entertain each other.

We set off, and, at first, delighted ourselves with the usual graceful motions of the arms. With what grace, with what ease, she moved! When the waltz commenced, and the dancers whirled around each other in the giddy maze, there was some confusion, owing to the incapacity of some of the dancers. We judiciously remained still, allowing the others to weary themselves; and, when the awkward dancers had withdrawn, we joined in, and kept it up famously together with one other couple, —Andran and his partner. Never did I dance more lightly. I felt myself more than mortal, holding this loveliest of creatures in my arms, flying, with her as rapidly as the wind, till I lost sight of every other object; and O Wilhelm, I vowed at that moment, that a maiden whom I loved, or for whom I felt the slightest attachment, never, never should waltz with anyone else but with me, if I went to perdition for it!—you will understand this.

We took a few turns in the room to recover our breath. Charlotte sat down and felt refreshed by partaking of some oranges which I had had secured, —the only ones that had been left; but at every slice which, from politeness, she offered to her neighbours, I felt as though a dagger went through my heart.

We were the second couple in the third country dance. As we were going down (and Heaven knows with what ecstasy I gazed at her arms and eyes, beaming with the sweetest feeling of pure and genuine enjoyment), we passed a lady whom I had noticed for her charming expression of countenance, although she was no longer young. She looked at Charlotte with a smile, then, holding up her finger in a threatening attitude, repeated twice in a very significant tone of voice the name of "Albert."

"Who is Albert," said I to Charlotte, "if it is not impertinent to ask?" She was about to answer, when we were obliged to separate, in order to execute a figure in the dance; and, as we crossed over again in front of each other, I perceived she looked somewhat pensive. "Why need I conceal it from you?" she said, as she gave me her hand for the promenade. "Albert is a worthy man, to whom I am engaged." Now, there was nothing new to me in this (for the girls had told me of it on the way); but it was so far new that I had not thought of it in connection with her whom, in so short a time, I had learned to prize so highly. Enough, I became confused, got out in the figure, and occasioned general confusion; so that it required all Charlotte's presence of mind to set me right by pulling and pushing me into my proper place.

The dance was not yet finished when the lightning which had for some time been seen in the horizon, and which I had asserted to proceed entirely from heat, grew more violent; and the thunder was heard above the music. When any distress or terror surprises us in the midst of our amusements, it naturally makes a deeper impression than at other times, either because the contrast makes us more keenly susceptible, or rather perhaps because our senses are then more open to impressions, and the shock is consequently stronger. To this cause, I must ascribe the fright and shrieks of the ladies. One sagaciously sat down in a corner with her back to the window, and held her fingers to her ears; a second knelt down before her, and hid her face in her lap; a third threw herself between them, and embraced her sister with a thousand tears; some insisted on going home; others, unconscious of their actions, wanted sufficient presence of mind to repress the impertinence of their young partners, who sought to direct to themselves those sighs which the lips of our agitated beauties intended for heaven. Some of the gentlemen had gone down-stairs to smoke a quiet cigar, and the rest of the company gladly embraced a happy suggestion of the hostess to retire into another room which was provided with shutters and curtains. We had hardly got there, when Charlotte placed the chairs in a circle; and, when the company had sat down in compliance with her request, she forthwith proposed a round game.

I noticed some of the company prepare their mouths and draw

themselves up at the prospect of some agreeable forfeit. "Let us play at counting," said Charlotte. "Now, pay attention: I shall go round the circle from right to left; and each person is to count, one after the other, the number that comes to him, and must count fast; whoever stops or mistakes is to have a box on the ear, and so on, till we have counted a thousand." It was delightful to see the fun. She went round the circle with upraised arm. "One," said the first; "two," the second; "three," the third; and so on, till Charlotte went faster and faster. One made a mistake, instantly a box on the ear; and, amid the laughter that ensued, came another box; and so on, faster, and faster. I myself came in for two. I fancied they were harder than the rest and felt quite delighted. A general laughter and confusion put an end to the game long before we had counted as far as a thousand. The party broke up into little separate knots: the storm had ceased, and I followed Charlotte into the ballroom. On the way she said, "The game banished their fears of the storm." I could make no reply. "I myself," she continued, "was as much frightened as any of them; but by affecting courage, to keep up the spirits of the others, I forgot my apprehensions." We went to the window. It was still thundering at a distance: a soft rain was pouring down over the country and filled the air around us with delicious odours. Charlotte leaned forward on her arm; her eyes wandered over the scene; she raised them to the sky, and then turned them upon me; they were moistened with tears; she placed her hand on mine and said, "Klopstock!" at once I remembered the magnificent ode which was in her thoughts: I felt oppressed with the weight of my sensations and sank under them. It was more than I could bear. I bent over her hand, kissed it in a stream of delicious tears, and again looked up to her eyes. Divine Klopstock! why didst thou not see thy apotheosis in those eyes? And thy name so often profaned, would that I never heard it repeated!

JUNE 19.

I no longer remember where I stopped in my narrative: I only know it was two in the morning when I went to bed; and if you had been with me, that I might have talked instead of writing to you, I should, in all probability, have kept you up till daylight.

I think I have not yet related what happened as we rode home from the ball, nor have I time to tell you now. It was a most magnificent sunrise: the whole country was refreshed, and the rain fell drop by drop from the trees in the forest. Our companions were asleep. Charlotte asked me if I did not wish to sleep also and begged of me not to make any ceremony on her account. Looking steadfastly at her, I answered, "As long as I see those eyes open, there is no fear of my falling asleep." We both continued awake till we reached her door. The maid opened it softly, and assured her, in answer to her inquiries, that her father and the children were well, and still sleeping. I left her asking permission to visit her in the course of the day. She consented, and I went, and, since that time, sun, moon, and stars may pursue their course: I know not whether it is day or night; the whole world is nothing to me.

JUNE 21.

My days are as happy as those reserved by God for his elect; and, whatever be my fate hereafter, I can never say that I have not tasted joy, —the purest joy of life. You know Walheim. I am now completely settled there. In that spot I am only half a league from Charlotte; and there I enjoy myself and taste all the pleasure which can fall to the lot of man.

Little did I imagine, when I selected Walheim for my pedestrian excursions, that all heaven lay so near it. How often in my wanderings from the hillside or from the meadows across the river, have I beheld this hunting-lodge, which now contains within it all the joy of my heart!

I have often, my dear Wilhelm, reflected on the eagerness men feel to wander and make new discoveries, and upon that secret impulse which afterward inclines them to return to their narrow circle, conform to the laws of custom, and embarrass themselves no longer with what passes around them.

It is so strange how, when I came here first, and gazed upon that lovely valley from the hillside, I felt charmed with the entire scene surrounding me. The little wood opposite—how delightful to sit under its shade! How fine the view from that point of rock! Then, that delightful chain of hills, and the exquisite valleys at their feet! Could I but wander and lose myself amongst them! I went and returned without finding what I wished. Distance, my friend, is like futurity. A dim vastness is spread before our souls: the perceptions of our mind are as obscure as those of our vision; and we desire earnestly to surrender up our whole being, that it may be filled with the complete and perfect bliss of one glorious emotion. But alas! when we have attained our object, when the distant there becomes the present here, all is changed: we are as poor and circumscribed as ever, and our souls still languish for unattainable happiness.

So does the restless traveller pant for his native soil, and find in his own cottage, in the arms of his wife, in the affections of his children, and in the labour necessary for their support, that happiness which he had sought in vain through the wide world.

When, in the morning at sunrise, I go out to Walheim, and with my own hands gather in the garden the Pease which are to serve for my dinner, when I sit down to shell them, and read my Homer during the intervals, and then, selecting a saucepan from the kitchen, fetch my own butter, put my mess on the fire, cover it up, and sit down to stir it as occasion requires, I figure to myself the illustrious suitors of Penelope, killing, dressing, and preparing their own oxen and swine. Nothing fills me with a more pure and genuine sense of happiness than those traits of patriarchal life which, thank Heaven! I can imitate without affectation. Happy is it, indeed, for me that my heart is capable of feeling the same simple and innocent pleasure as the peasant whose table is covered with food of his own rearing, and who not only enjoys his meal, but remembers with delight the happy days and sunny mornings when he planted it, the soft evenings when he watered it, and the pleasure he experienced in watching its daily growth.

JUNE 29.

The day before yesterday, the physician came from the town to pay a visit to the judge. He found me on the floor playing with Charlotte's children. Some of them were scrambling over me, and others romped with me; and, as I caught and tickled them, they made a great noise. The doctor is a formal sort of personage: he adjusts the plaits of his ruffles, and continually settles his frill whilst he is talking to you; and he thought my conduct beneath the dignity of a sensible man. I could perceive this by his countenance. But I did not suffer myself to be disturbed. I allowed him to continue his wise conversation, whilst I rebuilt the children's card houses for them as fast as they threw them down. He went about the town afterward, complaining that the judge's children were spoiled enough before, but that now Werther was completely ruining them.

Yes, my dear Wilhelm, nothing on this earth affects my heart so much as children. When I look on at their doings; when I mark in the little creatures the seeds of all those virtues and qualities which they will one day find so indispensable; when I behold in the obstinate all the future firmness and constancy of a noble character; in the capricious, that levity and gaiety of temper which will carry them lightly over the dangers and troubles of life, their whole nature simple and unpolluted,—then I call to mind the golden words of the Great Teacher of mankind, "Unless ye become like one of these!" And now, my friend, these children, who are our equals, whom we ought to consider as our models, we treat them as though they were our subjects. They are allowed no will of their own. And have we, then, none ourselves? Whence comes our exclusive right? Is it because we are older and more experienced? Great God! from the height of thy heaven thou beholdest great children and little children, and no others; and thy Son has long since declared which afford thee greatest pleasure. But they believe in him, and hear him not, —that, too, is an old story; and they train their children after their own image, etc.

Adieu, Wilhelm: I will not further bewilder myself with this subject.

JULY 1.

The consolation Charlotte can bring to an invalid I experience from my own heart, which suffers more from her absence than many a poor creature lingering on a bed of sickness. She is gone to spend a few days in the town with a very worthy woman, who is given over by the physicians, and wishes to have Charlotte near her in her last moments. I accompanied her last week on a visit to the Vicar of S—, a small village in the mountains, about a league hence. We arrived about four o'clock: Charlotte had taken her little sister with her. When we entered the vicarage court, we found the good old man sitting on a bench before the door, under the shade of two large walnut-trees. At the sight of Charlotte, he seemed to gain new life, rose, forgot his stick, and ventured to walk toward her. She ran to him, and made him sit down again; then, placing herself by his side, she gave him a number of messages from her father, and then caught up his youngest child, a dirty, ugly little thing, the joy of his old age, and kissed it. I wish you could have witnessed her attention to this old man,—how she raised her voice on account of his deafness; how she told him of healthy young people, who had been carried off when it was least expected; praised the virtues of Carlsbad, and commended his determination to spend the ensuing summer there; and assured him that he looked better and stronger than he did when she saw him last. I, in the meantime, paid attention to his good lady. The old man seemed quite in spirits; and as I could not help admiring the beauty of the walnut-trees, which formed such an agreeable shade over our heads, he began, though with some little difficulty, to tell us their history. "As to the oldest," said he, "we do not know who planted it, — some say one clergyman, and some another: but the younger one, there behind us, is exactly the age of my wife, fifty years old next October; her father planted it in the morning and in the evening, she came into the world. My wife's father was my predecessor here, and I cannot tell you how fond he was of that tree; and it is fully as dear to me. Under the shade of that very tree, upon a log of wood, my wife was seated knitting, when I, a poor student, came into this court for the first time, just seven and twenty years ago." Charlotte inquired for his daughter. He said she was gone with Herr Schmidt to the meadows and was with the haymakers. The old man then resumed his story and told us how his predecessor had taken a fancy to him, as had his daughter likewise; and how he had become first his curate, and subsequently his successor. He had scarcely finished his story when his daughter returned through the garden, accompanied by the above-mentioned Herr Schmidt. She welcomed Charlotte affectionately and I confess I was much taken with her appearance. She was a lively-looking, good-humoured brunette, quite competent to amuse one for a short time in the country. Her lover (for such Herr Schmidt evidently appeared to be) was a polite, reserved personage, and would not join our conversation, notwithstanding all Charlotte's endeavours to draw him out. I was much annoyed at observing, by his countenance, that his silence did not arise from want of talent, but from caprice and ill-humour. This subsequently became very evident, when we set out to take a walk, and Frederica joining Charlotte, with whom I was talking, the worthy gentleman's face, which was naturally rather sombre became so dark and angry that Charlotte was obliged to touch my arm and remind me that I was talking too much to Frederica. Nothing distresses me more than to see men torment each other; particularly when in the flower of their age, in the very season of pleasure, they waste their few short days of sunshine in quarrels and disputes, and only perceive their error when it is too late to repair it. This thought dwelt upon my mind; and in the evening, when we returned to the vicars, and were sitting round the table with our bread and milk, the conversation turned on the joys and sorrows of the world, I could not resist the temptation to inveigh bitterly against ill-humour. "We are apt," said I, "to complain, but—with very little cause, that our happy days are few, and our evil days many. If our hearts were always disposed to receive the benefits Heaven sends us, we should acquire strength to support evil when it comes." "But" observed the vicar's wife, "we cannot always command our tempers, so much depends upon the constitution: when the body suffers, the mind is ill at ease." "I acknowledge that," I continued; "but we must consider such a disposition in the light of a disease and inquire whether there is no remedy for it."

"I should be glad to hear one," said Charlotte: "at least, I think very much depends upon ourselves; I know it is so with me. When anything annoys me, and disturbs my temper, I hasten into the garden, hum a couple of country dances, and it is all right with me directly." "That is what I meant," I replied, "ill-humour resembles indolence: it is natural to us; but if once we have courage to exert ourselves, we find our work run fresh from our hands, and we experience in the activity from which we shrank a real enjoyment." Frederica listened very attentively, and the young man objected, that we were not masters of ourselves, and still less so of our feelings. "The question is about a disagreeable feeling," I added, "from which everyone would willingly escape, but none know their own power without trial. Invalids are glad to consult physicians, and submit to the most scrupulous regimen, the most nauseous medicines, in order to recover their health." I observed that the good old man inclined his head, and exerted himself to hear our discourse; so I raised my voice, and addressed myself directly to him. "We preach against a great many crimes,"

I observed, "but I never remember a sermon delivered against ill-humour." "That may do very well for your town clergymen," said he: "country people are never ill-humored; though, indeed, it might be useful, occasionally, to my wife for instance, and the judge." We all laughed, as did he likewise very cordially, till he fell into a fit of coughing, which interrupted our conversation for a time. Herr Schmidt resumed the subject. "You call ill humour a crime," he remarked, "but I think you use too strong a term." "Not at all," I replied, "if that deserves the name which is so pernicious to ourselves and our neighbours. Is it not enough that we want the power to make one another happy, must we deprive each other of the pleasure which we can all make for ourselves? Show me the man who has the courage to hide his ill-humour, who bears the whole burden himself, without disturbing the peace of those around him. No: ill-humour arises from an inward consciousness of our own want of merit, from a discontent which ever accompanies that envy which foolish vanity engenders. We see people happy, whom we have not made so, and cannot endure the sight." Charlotte looked at me with a smile; she observed the emotion with which I spoke: and a tear in the eyes of Frederica stimulated me to proceed. "Woe unto those," I said, "who use their power over a human heart to destroy the simple pleasures it would naturally enjoy! All the favours, all the attentions, in the world cannot compensate for the loss of that happiness which a cruel tyranny has destroyed." My heart was full as I spoke. A recollection of many things which had happened pressed upon my mind and filled my eyes with tears. "We should daily repeat to ourselves," I exclaimed, "that we should not interfere with our friends, unless to leave them in possession of their own joys and increase their happiness by sharing it with them! But when their souls are tormented by a violent passion, or their hearts rent with grief, is it in your power to afford them the slightest consolation?

"And when the last fatal malady seizes the being whose untimely grave you have prepared, when she lies languid and exhausted before you, her dim eyes raised to heaven, and the damp of death upon her pallid brow, there you stand at her bedside like a condemned criminal, with the bitter feeling that your whole fortune could not save her; and the agonizing thought wrings you, that all your efforts are powerless to impart even a moment's strength to the departing soul, or quicken her with a transitory consolation."

At these words the remembrance of a similar scene at which I had been once present fell with full force upon my heart. I buried my face in my handkerchief, and hastened from the room, and was only recalled to my recollection by Charlotte's voice, who reminded me that it was time to return home. With what tenderness she chid me on the way for the too eager interest I took in everything! She declared it would do me injury, and that I ought to spare myself. Yes, my angel! I will do so for your sake.

JULY 6.

She is still with her dying friend, and is still the same bright, beautiful creature whose presence softens pain, and sheds happiness around whichever way she turns. She went out yesterday with her little sisters: I knew it and went to meet them; and we walked together. In about an hour and a half we returned to the town. We stopped at the spring I am so fond of, and which is now a thousand times dearer to me than ever. Charlotte seated herself upon the low wall, and we gathered about her. I looked around, and recalled the time when my heart was unoccupied and free. "Dear fountain!" I said, "since that time I have no more come to enjoy cool repose by thy fresh stream: I have passed thee with careless steps and scarcely bestowed a glance upon thee." I looked down, and observed Charlotte's little sister, Jane, coming up the steps with a glass of water. I turned toward Charlotte, and I felt her influence over me. Jane at the moment approached with the glass. Her sister, Marianne, wished to take it from her. "No!" cried the child, with the sweetest expression of face, "Charlotte must drink first."

The affection and simplicity with which this was uttered so charmed me, that I sought to express my feelings by catching up the child and kissing her heartily. She was frightened and began to cry. "You should not do that," said Charlotte: I felt perplexed. "Come, Jane," she continued, taking her hand, and leading her down the steps again, "it is no matter: wash yourself quickly in the fresh water." I stood and watched them; and when I saw the little dear rubbing her cheeks with her wet hands, in full belief that all the impurities contracted from my ugly beard would be washed off by the miraculous water, and how, though Charlotte said it would do, she continued still to wash with all her might, as though she thought too much were better than too little, I assure you, Wilhelm, I never attended a baptism with greater reverence; and, when Charlotte came up from the well, I could have prostrated myself as before the prophet of an Eastern nation.

In the evening I would not resist telling the story to a person who, I thought, possessed some natural feeling, because he was a man of understanding. But what a mistake I made. He maintained it was very wrong of Charlotte, that we should not deceive children, that such things occasioned countless mistakes and superstitions, from which we were bound to protect the young. It occurred to me then, that this very man had been baptized only a week before; so, I said nothing further, but maintained the justice of my own convictions. We should deal with children as God deals with us, we are happiest under the influence of innocent delusions.

JULY 8.

What a child is man that he should be so solicitous about a look! What a child is man! We had been to Walheim: the ladies went in a carriage; but during our walk I thought I saw in Charlotte's dark eyes—I am a fool—but forgive me! you should see them,—those eyes.—However, to be brief (for my own eyes are weighed down with sleep), you must know, when the ladies stepped into their carriage again, young W. Seldstadt, Andran, and I were standing about the door. They are a merry set of fellows, and they were all laughing and joking together. I watched Charlotte's eyes. They wandered from one to the other; but they did not light on me, on me, who stood there motionless, and who saw nothing but her! My heart bade her a thousand times adieu, but she noticed me not. The carriage drove off; and my eyes filled with tears. I looked after her: suddenly I saw Charlotte's bonnet leaning out of the window, and she turned to look back, was it at me? My dear friend, I know not; and in this uncertainty I find consolation. Perhaps she turned to look at me. Perhaps! Good-night—what a child I am!

JULY 10.

You should see how foolish I look in company when her name is mentioned, particularly when I am asked plainly how I like her. How I like her! I detest the phrase. What sort of creature must he be who merely liked Charlotte, whose whole heart and senses were not entirely absorbed by her. Like her! Someone asked me lately how I liked Ossian.

JULY 11.

Madame M—is very ill. I pray for her recovery because Charlotte shares my sufferings. I see her occasionally at my friend's house, and today she has told me the strangest circumstance. Old M—is a covetous, miserly fellow, who has long worried and annoyed the poor lady sadly; but she has borne her afflictions patiently. A few days ago, when the physician informed us that her recovery was hopeless, she sent for her husband (Charlotte was present) and addressed him thus: "I have something to confess, which, after my decease, may occasion trouble and confusion. I have hitherto conducted your household as frugally and economically as possible, but you must pardon me for having defrauded you for thirty years. At the commencement of our married life, you allowed a small sum for the wants of the kitchen, and the other household expenses. When our establishment increased and our property grew larger, I could not persuade you to increase the weekly allowance in proportion: in short, you know, that, when our wants were greatest, you required me to supply everything with seven florins a week. I took the money from you without an observation but made up the weekly deficiency from the money-chest as nobody would suspect your wife of robbing the household bank. But I have wasted nothing and should have been content to meet my eternal Judge without this confession, if she, upon whom the management of your establishment will devolve after my decease, would be free from embarrassment upon your insisting that the allowance made to me, your former wife, was sufficient."

I talked with Charlotte of the inconceivable manner in which men allow themselves to be blinded; how anyone could avoid suspecting some deception, when seven florins only were allowed to defray expenses twice as great. But I have myself known people who believed, without any visible astonishment, that their house possessed the prophet's never-failing cruse of oil.

JULY 13.

No, I am not deceived. In her dark eyes I read a genuine interest in me and in my fortunes. Yes, I feel it; and I may believe my own heart which tells me—dare I say it? —dare I pronounce the divine words? —that she loves me!

That she loves me! How the idea exalts me in my own eyes! And, as you can understand my feelings, I may say to you, how I honour myself since she loves me!

Is this presumption, or is it a consciousness of the truth? I do not know a man able to supplant me in the heart of Charlotte; and yet when she speaks of her betrothed with so much warmth and affection, I feel like the soldier who has been stripped of his honours and titles and deprived of his sword.

JULY 16.

How my heart beats when by accident I touch her finger, or my feet meet hers under the table! I draw back as if from a furnace; but a secret force impels me forward again, and my senses become disordered. Her innocent, unconscious heart never knows what agony these little familiarities inflict upon me. Sometimes when we are talking, she lays her hand upon mine, and in the eagerness of conversation comes closer to me and her balmy breath reaches my lips, —when I feel as if lightning had struck me, and that I could sink into the earth. And yet, Wilhelm, with all this heavenly confidence, —if I know myself, and should ever dare—you understand me. No, no! my heart is not so corrupt, it is weak, weak enough but is not that a degree of corruption?

She is to me a sacred being. All passion is still in her presence: I cannot express my sensations when I am near her. I feel as if my soul beat in every nerve of my body. There is a melody which she plays on the piano with angelic skill, —so simple is it, and yet so spiritual! It is her favourite air; and, when she plays the first note, all pain, care, and sorrow disappear from me in a moment.

I believe every word that is said of the magic of ancient music. How her simple song enchants me! Sometimes, when I am ready to commit suicide, she sings that air; and instantly the gloom and madness which hung over me are dispersed, and I breathe freely again.

JULY 18.

Wilhelm, what is the world to our hearts without love? What is a magic-lantern without light? You have but to kindle the flame within, and the brightest figures shine on the white wall; and, if love only show us fleeting shadows, we are yet happy, when, like mere children, we behold them, and are transported with the splendid phantoms. I have not been able to see Charlotte today. I was prevented by company from which I could not disengage myself. What was to be done? I sent my servant to her house, that I might at least see somebody to-day who had been near her. Oh, the impatience with which I waited for his return! the joy with which I welcomed him! I should certainly have caught him in my arms, and kissed him, if I had not been ashamed.

It is said that the Bonona stone, when placed in the sun, attracts the rays, and for a time appears luminous in the dark. So was it with me and this servant. The idea that Charlotte's eyes had dwelt on his countenance, his cheek, his very apparel, endeared them all inestimably to me, so that at the moment I would not have parted from him for a thousand crowns. His presence made me so happy! Beware of laughing at me, Wilhelm. Can that be a delusion which makes us happy?

JULY 19.

"I shall see her today!" I exclaim with delight, when I rise in the morning, and look out with gladness of heart at the bright, beautiful sun. "I shall see her today!" And then I have no further wish to form, all, all is included in that one thought.

JULY 20.

I cannot assent to your proposal that I should accompany the ambassador to ———. I do not love subordination; and we all know that he is a rough, disagreeable person to be connected with. You say my mother wishes me to be employed. I could not help laughing at that. Am I not sufficiently employed? And is it not in reality the same, whether I shell peas or count lentils? The world runs on from one folly to another; and the man who, solely from regard to the opinion of others, and without any wish or necessity of his own, toils after gold, honour, or any other phantom, is no better than a fool.

JULY 24.

You insist so much on my not neglecting my drawing, that it would be as well for me to say nothing as to confess how little I have lately done.

I never felt happier, I never understood nature better, even down to the veriest stem or smallest blade of grass; and yet I am unable to express myself: my powers of execution are so weak, everything seems to swim and float before me, so that I cannot make a clear, bold outline. But I fancy I should succeed better if I had some clay or wax to model. I shall try, if this state of mind continues much longer, and will take to modelling, if I only knead dough.

I have commenced Charlotte's portrait three times and have as often disgraced myself. This is the more annoying, as I was formerly very happy in taking likenesses. I have since sketched her profile and must content myself with that.

JULY 25.

Yes, dear Charlotte! I will order and arrange everything. Only give me more commissions, the more the better. One thing, however, I must request: use no more writing-sand with the dear notes you send me. Today I raised your letter hastily to my lips, and it set my teeth on edge.

JULY 26.

I have often determined not to see her so frequently. But who could keep such a resolution? Every day I am exposed to the temptation and promise faithfully that tomorrow I will really stay away but when tomorrow comes, I find some irresistible reason for seeing her; and, before I can account for it, I am with her again. Either she has said on the previous evening "You will be sure to call to-morrow,"—and who could stay away then?—or she gives me some commission and I find it essential to take her the answer in person; or the day is fine, and I walk to Walheim; and, when I am there, it is only half a league farther to her. I am within the charmed atmosphere, and soon find myself at her side. My grandmother used to tell us a story of a mountain of loadstone. When any vessels came near it, they were instantly deprived of their ironwork: the nails flew to the mountain, and the unhappy crew perished amidst the disjointed planks.

JULY 30.

Albert is arrived, and I must take my departure. Were he the best and noblest of men, and I in every respect his inferior, I could not endure to see him in possession of such a perfect being. Possession! —enough, Wilhelm: her betrothed is here, —a fine, worthy fellow, whom one cannot help liking. Fortunately, I was not present at their meeting. It would have broken my heart! And he is so considerate: he has not given Charlotte one kiss in my presence. Heaven reward him for it! I must love him for the respect with which he treats her. He shows a regard for me, but for this I suspect I am more indebted to Charlotte than to his own fancy for me. Women have a delicate tact in such matters, and it should be so. They cannot always succeed in keeping two rivals on terms with each other; but, when they do, they are the only gainers.

I cannot help esteeming Albert. The coolness of his temper contrasts strongly with the impetuosity of mine, which I cannot conceal. He has a great deal of feeling and is fully sensible of the treasure he possesses in Charlotte. He is free from ill-humour, which you know is the fault I detest most.

He regards me as a man of sense and my attachment to Charlotte, and the interest I take in all that concerns her, augment his triumph and his love. I shall not inquire whether he may not at times tease her with some little jealousies; as I know, that, were I in his place, I should not be entirely free from such sensations.

But be that as it may, my pleasure with Charlotte is over. Call it folly or infatuation, what signifies a name? The thing speaks for itself. Before Albert came, I knew all that I know now. I knew I could make no pretensions to her, nor did I offer any, that is, as far as it was possible, in the presence of so much loveliness, not to pant for its enjoyment. And now, behold me like a silly fellow, staring with astonishment when another comes in, and deprives me of my love.

I bite my lips and feel infinite scorn for those who tell me to be resigned, because there is no help for it. Let me escape from the yoke of such silly subterfuges! I ramble through the woods; and when I return to Charlotte and find Albert sitting by her side in the summerhouse in the garden, I am unable to bear it, behave like a fool, and commit a thousand extravagances. "For Heaven's sake," said Charlotte today, "let us have no more scenes like those of last night! You terrify me when you are so violent." Between ourselves, I am always away now when he visits her: and I feel delighted when I find her alone.

AUGUST 8.

Believe me, dear Wilhelm, I did not allude to you when I spoke so severely of those who advise resignation to inevitable fate. I did not think it possible for you to indulge such a sentiment. But in fact, you are right. I only suggest one objection. In this world one is seldom reduced to make a selection between two alternatives. There are as many varieties of conduct and opinion as there are turns of feature between an aquiline nose and a flat one.

You will, therefore, permit me to concede your entire argument, and yet contrive means to escape your dilemma.

Your position is this, I hear you say: "Either you have hopes of obtaining Charlotte, or you have none. Well, in the first case, pursue your course, and press on to the fulfilment of your wishes. In the second, be a man, and shake off a miserable passion, which will enervate and destroy you." My dear friend, this is well and easily said.

But would you require a wretched being, whose life is slowly wasting under a lingering disease, to dispatch himself at once by the stroke of a dagger? Does not the very disorder which consumes his strength deprive him of the courage to effect his deliverance?

You may answer me, if you please, with a similar analogy, "Who would not prefer the amputation of an arm to the periling of life by doubt and procrastination!" But I know not if I am right and let us leave these comparisons.

Enough! There are moments, Wilhelm, when I could rise up and shake it all off, and when, if I only knew where to go, I could fly from this place.

THE SAME EVENING.

My diary, which I have for some time neglected, came before me today; and I am amazed to see how deliberately I have entangled myself step by step. To have seen my position so clearly and yet to have acted so like a child! Even still I behold the result plainly, and yet have no thought of acting with greater prudence.

AUGUST 10.

If I were not a fool, I could spend the happiest and most delightful life here. So many agreeable circumstances, and of a kind to ensure a worthy man's happiness, are seldom united. Alas! I feel it too sensibly, —the heart alone makes our happiness! To be admitted into this most charming family, to be loved by the father as a son, by the children as a father, and by Charlotte! then the noble Albert, who never disturbs my happiness by any appearance of ill-humour, receiving me with the heartiest affection, and loving me, next to Charlotte, better than all the world! Wilhelm, you would be delighted to hear us in our rambles, and conversations about Charlotte. Nothing in the world can be more absurd than our connection, and yet the thought of it often moves me to tears.

He tells me sometimes of her excellent mother; how, upon her death-bed, she had committed her house and children to Charlotte, and had given Charlotte herself in charge to him; how, since that time, a new spirit had taken possession of her; how, in care and anxiety for their welfare, she became a real mother to them; how every moment of her time was devoted to some labour of love in their behalf, —and yet her mirth and cheerfulness had never forsaken her. I walk by his side, pluck flowers by the way, arrange them carefully into a nosegay, then fling them into the first stream I pass, and watch them as they float gently away. I forget whether I told you that Albert is to remain here. He has received a government appointment, with a very good salary; and I understand he is in high favour at court. I have met few persons so punctual and methodical in business.

AUGUST 12.

Certainly, Albert is the best fellow in the world. I had a strange scene with him yesterday. I went to take leave of him; for I took it into my head to spend a few days in these mountains, from where I now write to you. As I was walking up and down his room, my eye fell upon his pistols. "Lend me those pistols," said I, "for my journey." "By all means," he replied, "if you will take the trouble to load them; for they only hang there for form." I took down one of them; and he continued, "Ever since I was near suffering for my extreme caution, I will have nothing to do with such things." I was curious to hear the story. "I was staying," said he, "some three months ago, at a friend's house in the country. I had a brace of pistols with me, unloaded; and I slept without any anxiety. One rainy afternoon I was sitting by myself, doing nothing, when it occurred to me, I do not know how that the house might be attacked, that we might require the pistols, that we might in short, you know how we go on fancying, when we have nothing better to do. I gave the pistols to the servant, to clean and load. He was playing with the maid, and trying to frighten her, when the pistol went off—God knows how! —the ramrod was in the barrel; and it went straight through her right hand and shattered the thumb. I had to endure all the lamentation, and to pay the surgeon's bill; so, since that time, I have kept all my weapons unloaded. But, my dear friend, what is the use of prudence? We can never be on our guard against all possible dangers. However,"—now, you must know I can tolerate all men till they come to "however;"—for it is self-evident that every universal rule must have its exceptions. But he is so exceedingly accurate, that, if he only fancies, he has said a word too precipitate, or too general, or only half true, he never ceases to qualify, to modify, and extenuate, till at last he appears to have said nothing at all. Upon this occasion, Albert was deeply immersed in his subject: I ceased to listen to him and became lost in reverie. With a sudden motion, I pointed the mouth of the pistol to my forehead, over the right eye. "What do you mean?" cried Albert, turning back the pistol. "It is not loaded," said I. "And even if not," he answered with impatience, "what can you mean? I cannot comprehend how a man can be so mad as to shoot himself, and the bare idea of it shocks me."

"But why should anyone," said I, "in speaking of an action, venture to pronounce it mad or wise, or good or bad? What is the meaning of all this? Have you carefully studied the secret motives of our actions? Do you understand—can you explain the causes which occasion them and make them inevitable? If you can, you will be less hasty with your decision."

"But you will allow," said Albert; "that some actions are criminal, let them spring from whatever motives they may." I granted it and shrugged my shoulders.

"But still, my good friend," I continued, "there are some exceptions here too. Theft is a crime; but the man who commits it from extreme poverty, with no design but to save his family from perishing, is he an object of pity, or of punishment? Who shall throw the first stone at a husband, who, in the heat of just resentment, sacrifices his faithless wife and her perfidious seducer? or at the young maiden, who, in her weak hour of rapture, forgets herself in the impetuous joys of love? Even our laws, cold and cruel as they are, relent in such cases, and withhold their punishment."

"That is quite another thing," said Albert; "because a man under the influence of violent passion loses all power of reflection and is regarded as intoxicated or insane."

"Oh! you people of sound understandings," I replied, smiling, "are ever ready to exclaim 'Extravagance, and madness, and intoxication!' You moral men are so calm and so subdued! You abhor the drunken man, and detest the extravagant; you pass by, like the Levite, and thank God, like the Pharisee, that you are not like one of them. I have been more than once intoxicated, my passions have always bordered on extravagance: I am not ashamed to confess it; for I have learned, by my own experience, that all extraordinary men, who have accomplished great and astonishing actions, have ever been decried by the world as drunken or insane. And in private life, too, is it not intolerable that no one can undertake the execution of a noble or generous deed, without giving rise to the exclamation that the doer is intoxicated or mad? Shame upon you, ye sages!"

"This is another of your extravagant humours," said Albert: "you always exaggerate a case, and in this matter, you are undoubtedly wrong; for we were speaking of suicide, which you compare with great actions, when it is impossible to regard it as anything but a weakness. It is much easier to die than to bear a life of misery with fortitude."

I was on the point of breaking off the conversation, for nothing puts me so completely out of patience as the utterance of a wretched commonplace when I am talking from my inmost heart. However, I composed myself, for I had often heard the same observation with sufficient vexation; and I answered him, therefore, with a little warmth, "You call this a weakness—beware of being led astray by appearances. When a nation, which has long groaned under the intolerable yoke of a tyrant, rises at last and throws off its chains, do you call that weakness? The man who, to rescue his house from the flames, finds his physical strength redoubled, so that he lifts burdens with ease, which, in the absence of excitement, he could scarcely move; he who, under the rage of an insult, attacks and puts to flight half a score of his enemies, are such persons to be called weak? My good friend, if resistance be strength, how can the highest degree of resistance be a weakness?"

Albert looked steadfastly at me, and said, "Pray forgive me, but I do not see that the examples you have adduced bear any relation to the question." "Very likely," I answered, "for I have often been told that my style of illustration borders a little on the absurd. But let us see if we cannot place the matter in another point of view, by inquiring what can be a man's state of mind who resolves to free himself from the burden of life, —a burden often so pleasant to bear, —for we cannot otherwise reason fairly upon the subject.

"Human nature," I continued, "has its limits. It is able to endure a certain degree of joy, sorrow, and pain, but becomes annihilated as soon as this measure is exceeded. The question, therefore, is, not whether a man is strong or weak, but whether he is able to endure the measure of his sufferings. The suffering may be moral or physical; and in my opinion it is just as absurd to call a man a coward who destroys himself, as to call a man a coward who dies of a malignant fever."

"Paradox, all paradox!" exclaimed Albert. "Not so paradoxical as you imagine," I replied. "You allow that we designate a disease as mortal when nature is so severely attacked, and her strength so far exhausted, that she cannot possibly recover her former condition under any change that may take place.

"Now, my good friend, apply this to the mind; observe a man in his natural, isolated condition; consider how ideas work, and how impressions fasten on him, till at length a violent passion seizes him, destroying all his powers of calm reflection, and utterly ruining him.

"It is in vain that a man of sound mind and cool temper understands the condition of such a wretched being, in vain he counsels him. He can no more communicate his own wisdom to him than a healthy man can instill his strength into the invalid, by whose bedside he is seated."

Albert thought this too general. I reminded him of a girl who had drowned herself a short time previously, and I related her history.

She was a good creature, who had grown up in the narrow sphere of household industry and weekly appointed labour; one who knew no pleasure beyond indulging in a walk on Sundays, arrayed in her best attire, accompanied by her friends, or perhaps joining in the dance now and then at some festival, and chatting away her spare hours with a neighbour, discussing the scandal or the quarrels of the village, trifles sufficient to occupy her heart. At length the warmth of her nature is influenced by certain new and unknown wishes. Inflamed by the flatteries of men, her former pleasures become by degrees insipid, till at length she meets with a youth to whom she is attracted by an indescribable feeling; upon him she now rests all her hopes; she forgets the world around her; she sees, hears, desires nothing but him, and him only. He alone occupies all her thoughts. Uncorrupted by the idle indulgence of an enervating vanity, her affection moving steadily toward its object, she hopes to become his, and to realize, in an everlasting union with him, all that happiness which she sought, all that bliss for which she longed. His repeated promises confirm her hopes, embraces and endearments, which increase the ardour of her desires, overmaster her soul. She floats in a dim, delusive anticipation of her happiness; and her feelings become excited to their utmost tension. She stretches out her arms finally to embrace the object of all her wishes and her lover forsakes her. Stunned and bewildered, she stands upon a precipice. All is darkness around her. No prospect, no hope, no consolation—forsaken by him in whom her existence was centered! She sees nothing of the wide world before her, thinks nothing of the many individuals who might supply the void in her heart; she feels herself deserted, forsaken by the world; and, blinded and impelled by the agony which wrings her soul, she plunges into the deep, to end her sufferings in the broad embrace of death. See here, Albert, the history of thousands; and tell me, is not this a case of physical infirmity? Nature has no way to escape from the labyrinth: her powers are exhausted: she can contend no longer, and the poor soul must die.

"Shame upon him who can look on calmly, and exclaim, 'The foolish girl! she should have waited; she should have allowed time to wear off the impression; her despair would have been softened, and she would have found another lover to comfort her.' One might as well say, 'The fool, to die of a fever! why did he not wait till his strength was restored, till his blood became calm? all would then have gone well, and he would have been alive now.'"

Albert, who could not see the justice of the comparison, offered some further objections, and, amongst others, urged that I had taken the case of a mere ignorant girl. But how any man of sense, of more enlarged views and experience, could be excused, he was unable to comprehend. "My friend!" I exclaimed, "man is but man; and, whatever be the extent of his reasoning powers, they are of little avail when passion rages within, and he feels himself confined by the narrow limits of nature. It were better, then—but we will talk of this some other time," I said, and caught up my hat. Alas! my heart was full; and we parted without conviction on either side. How rarely in this world do men understand each other!

AUGUST 15.

There can be no doubt that in this world nothing is so indispensable as love. I observe that Charlotte could not lose me without a pang, and the very children have but one wish; that is, that I should visit them again tomorrow. I went this afternoon to tune Charlotte's piano. But I could not do it, for the little ones insisted on my telling them a story; and Charlotte herself urged me to satisfy them. I waited upon them at tea, and they are now as fully contented with me as with Charlotte; and I told them my very best tale of the princess who was waited upon by dwarfs. I improve myself by this exercise and am quite surprised at the impression my stories create. If I sometimes invent an incident which I forget upon the next narration, they remind one directly that the story was different before; so that I now endeavour to relate with exactness the same anecdote in the same monotonous tone, which never changes. I find by this, how much an author injures his works by altering them, even though they be improved in a poetical point of view. The first impression is readily received. We are so constituted that we believe the most incredible things; and, once they are engraved upon the memory, woe to him who would endeavour to efface them.

AUGUST 18.

Must it ever be thus, —that the source of our happiness must also be the fountain of our misery? The full and ardent sentiment which animated my heart with the love of nature, overwhelming me with a torrent of delight, and which brought all paradise before me, has now become an insupportable torment, a demon which perpetually pursues and harasses me. When in bygone days I gazed from these rocks upon yonder mountains across the river, and upon the green, flowery valley before me, and saw all nature budding and bursting around; the hills clothed from foot to peak with tall, thick forest trees; the valleys in all their varied windings, shaded with the loveliest woods; and the soft river gliding along amongst the lisping reeds, mirroring the beautiful clouds which the soft evening breeze wafted across the sky, —when I heard the groves about me melodious with the music of birds, and saw the million swarms of insects dancing in the last golden beams of the sun, whose setting rays awoke the humming beetles from their grassy beds, whilst the subdued tumult around directed my attention to the ground, and I there observed the arid rock compelled to yield nutriment to the dry moss, whilst the heath flourished upon the barren sands below me, all this displayed to me the inner warmth which animates all nature, and filled and glowed within my heart. I felt myself exalted by this overflowing fulness to the perception of the Godhead, and the glorious forms of an infinite universe became visible to my soul! Stupendous mountains encompassed me, abysses yawned at my feet, and cataracts fell headlong down before me; impetuous rivers rolled through the plain, and rocks and mountains resounded from afar. In the depths of the earth, I saw innumerable powers in motion, and multiplying to infinity; whilst upon its surface, and beneath the heavens, there teemed ten thousand varieties of living creatures. Everything around is alive with an infinite number of forms; while mankind fly for security to their petty houses, from the shelter of which they rule in their imaginations over the wide-extended universe. Poor fool! in whose petty estimation all things are little. From the inaccessible mountains, across the desert which no mortal foot has trod, far as the confines of the unknown ocean, breathes the spirit of the eternal Creator; and every atom to which he has given existence finds favour in his sight. Ah, how often at that time has the flight of a bird, soaring above my head, inspired me with the desire of being transported to the shores of the immeasurable waters, there to quaff the pleasures of life from the foaming goblet of the Infinite, and to partake, if but for a moment even, with the confined powers of my soul, the beatitude of that Creator who accomplishes all things in himself, and through himself!

My dear friend, the bare recollection of those hours still consoles me. Even this effort to recall those ineffable sensations and give them utterance, exalts my soul above itself, and makes me doubly feel the intensity of my present anguish.

It is as if a curtain had been drawn from before my eyes, and, instead of prospects of eternal life, the abyss of an ever-open grave yawned before me. Can we say of anything that it exists when all passes away, when time, with the speed of a storm, carries all things onward, —and our transitory existence, hurried along by the torrent, is either swallowed up by the waves or dashed against the rocks? There is not a moment but preys upon you, —and upon all around you, not a moment in which you do not yourself become a destroyer. The most innocent walk deprives of life thousands of poor insects: one step destroys the fabric of the industrious ant and converts a little world into chaos. No: it is not the great and rare calamities of the world, the floods which sweep away whole villages, the earthquakes which swallow up our towns, that affect me. My heart is wasted by the thought of that destructive power which lies concealed in every part of universal nature. Nature has formed nothing that does not consume itself, and every object near it: so that, surrounded by earth and air, and all the active powers, I wander on my way with aching heart; and the universe is to me a fearful monster, forever devouring its own offspring.

AUGUST 21.

In vain do I stretch out my arms toward her when I awaken in the morning from my weary slumbers. In vain do I seek for her at night in my bed, when some innocent dream has happily deceived me, and placed her near me in the fields, when I have seized her hand and covered it with countless kisses. And when I feel for her in the half confusion of sleep, with the happy sense that she is near, tears flow from my oppressed heart and bereft of all comfort, I weep over my future woes.

AUGUST 22.

What a misfortune, Wilhelm! My active spirits have degenerated into contented indolence. I cannot be idle, and yet I am unable to set to work. I cannot think, I have no longer any feeling for the beauties of nature, and books are distasteful to me. Once we give ourselves up, we are totally lost. Many a time and oft I wish I were a common labourer; that, awakening in the morning, I might have but one prospect, one pursuit, one hope, for the day which has dawned. I often envy Albert when I see him buried in a heap of papers and parchments and I fancy I should be happy were I in his place. Often impressed with this feeling I have been on the point of writing to you and to the minister, for the appointment at the embassy, which you think I might obtain. I believe I might procure it. The minister has long shown a regard for me and has frequently urged me to seek employment. It is the business of an hour only. Now and then the fable of the horse recurs to me. Weary of liberty, he suffered himself to be saddled and bridled, and was ridden to death for his pains. I know not what to determine upon. For is not this anxiety for change the consequence of that restless spirit which would pursue me equally in every situation of life?

AUGUST 28.

If my ills would admit of any cure, they would certainly be cured here. This is my birthday, and early in the morning I received a packet from Albert. Upon opening it, I found one of the pink ribbons which Charlotte wore in her dress the first time I saw her, and which I had several times asked her to give me. With it were two volumes in duodecimo of Wetstein's "Homer," a book I had often wished for, to save me the inconvenience of carrying the large Ernestine edition with me upon my walks. You see how they anticipate my wishes, how well they understand all those little attentions of friendship, so superior to the costly presents of the great, which are humiliating. I kissed the ribbon a thousand times, and in every breath inhaled the remembrance of those happy and irrevocable days which filled me with the keenest joy. Such, Wilhelm, is our fate. I do not murmur at it: the flowers of life are but visionary. How many pass away and leave no trace behind—how few yield any fruit—and the fruit itself, how rarely does it ripen! And yet there are flowers enough! and is it not strange, my friend, that we should suffer the little that does really ripen, to rot, decay, and perish unenjoyed? Farewell! This is a glorious summer. I often climb into the trees in Charlotte's orchard and shake down the pears that hang on the highest branches. She stands below and catches them as they fall.

AUGUST 30.

Unhappy being that I am! Why do I thus deceive myself? What is to come of all this wild, aimless, endless passion? I cannot pray except to her. My imagination sees nothing but her: all surrounding objects are of no account, except as they relate to her. In this dreamy state I enjoy many happy hours, till at length I feel compelled to tear myself away from her. Ah, Wilhelm, to what does not my heart often compel me! When I have spent several hours in her company, till I feel completely absorbed by her figure, her grace, the divine expression of her thoughts, my mind becomes gradually excited to the highest excess, my sight grows dim, my hearing confused, my breathing oppressed as if by the hand of a murderer, and my beating heart seeks to obtain relief for my aching senses. I am sometimes unconscious whether I really exist. If in such moments I find no sympathy, and Charlotte does not allow me to enjoy the melancholy consolation of bathing her hand with my tears, I feel compelled to tear myself from her, when I either wander through the country, climb some precipitous cliff, or force a path through the trackless thicket, where I am lacerated and torn by thorns and briers; and thence I find relief. Sometimes I lie stretched on the ground, overcome with fatigue, and dying with thirst; sometimes, late in the night, when the moon shines above me, I recline against an aged tree in some sequestered forest, to rest my weary limbs, when, exhausted and worn, I sleep till break of day. O Wilhelm! the hermit's cell, his sackcloth, and girdle of thorns would be luxury and indulgence compared with what I suffer. Adieu! I see no end to this wretchedness except the grave.

SEPTEMBER 3.

I must away. Thank you, Wilhelm, for determining my wavering purpose. For a whole fortnight I have thought of leaving her. I must away. She has returned to town and is at the house of a friend. And then, Albert—yes, I must go.

SEPTEMBER 10.

Oh, what a night, Wilhelm! I can henceforth bear anything. I shall never see her again. Oh, why cannot I fall on your neck, and, with floods of tears and raptures, give utterance to all the passions which distract my heart! Here I sit gasping for breath and struggling to compose myself. I wait for day, and at sunrise the horses are to be at the door.

And she is sleeping calmly, little suspecting that she has seen me for the last time. I am free. I have had the courage, in an interview of two hours' duration, not to betray my intention. And O Wilhelm, what a conversation it was!

Albert had promised to come to Charlotte in the garden immediately after supper. I was upon the terrace under the tall chestnut trees and watched the setting sun. I saw him sink for the last time beneath this delightful valley and silent stream. I had often visited the same spot with Charlotte and witnessed that glorious sight; and now—I was walking up and down the very avenue which was so dear to me. A secret sympathy had frequently drawn me thither before I knew Charlotte; and we were delighted when, in our early acquaintance, we discovered that we each loved the same spot, which is indeed as romantic as any that ever captivated the fancy of an artist.

From beneath the chestnut trees, there is an extensive view. But I remember that I have mentioned all this in a former letter and have described the tall mass of beech trees at the end, and how the avenue grows darker and darker as it winds its way among them, till it ends in a gloomy recess, which has all the charm of a mysterious solitude. I still remember the strange feeling of melancholy which came over me the first time I entered that dark retreat, at bright midday. I felt some secret foreboding that it would, one day, be to me the scene of some happiness or misery.

I had spent half an hour struggling between the contending thoughts of going and returning when I heard them coming up the terrace. I ran to meet them. I trembled as I took her hand and kissed it. As we reached the top of the terrace, the moon rose from behind the wooded hill. We conversed on many subjects, and, without perceiving it, approached the gloomy recess. Charlotte entered and sat down. Albert seated himself beside her. I did the same, but my agitation did not suffer me to remain long seated. I got up, and stood before her, then walked backward and forward, and sat down again. I was restless and miserable. Charlotte drew our attention to the beautiful effect of the moonlight, which threw a silver hue over the terrace in front of us, beyond the beech trees. It was a glorious sight and was rendered more striking by the darkness which surrounded the spot where we were. We remained for some time silent, when Charlotte observed, "Whenever I walk by moonlight, it brings to my remembrance all my beloved and departed friends, and I am filled with thoughts of death and futurity. We shall live again, Werther!" she continued, with a firm but feeling voice; "but shall we know one another again what do you think? what do you say?"

"Charlotte," I said, as I took her hand in mine, and my eyes filled with tears, "we shall see each other again—here and hereafter we shall meet again." I could say no more. Why, Wilhelm, should she put this question to me, just at the moment when the fear of our cruel separation filled my heart?

"And oh! do those departed ones know how we are employed here? do they know when we are well and happy? do they know when we recall their memories with the fondest love? In the silent hour of evening the shade of my mother hovers around me; when seated in the midst of my children, I see them assembled near me, as they used to assemble near her; and then I raise my anxious eyes to heaven, and wish she could look down upon us, and witness how I fulfil the promise I made to her in her last moments, to be a mother to her children. With what emotion do I then exclaim, 'Pardon, dearest of mothers, pardon me, if I do not adequately supply your place! Alas! I do my utmost. They are clothed and fed; and, still better, they are loved and educated. Could you but see, sweet saint! the peace and harmony that dwells amongst us, you would glorify God with the warmest feelings of gratitude, to whom, in your last hour, you addressed such fervent prayers for our happiness.'" Thus, did she express herself; but O Wilhelm! who can do justice to her language? how can cold and passionless words convey the heavenly expressions of the spirit? Albert interrupted her gently. "This affects you too deeply, my dear Charlotte. I know your soul dwells on such recollections with intense delight; but I implore—" "O Albert!" she continued, "I am sure you do not forget the evenings when we three used to sit at the little round table, when papa was absent, and the little ones had retired. You often had a good book with you, but seldom read it; the conversation of that noble being was preferable to everything, —that beautiful, bright, gentle, and yet ever-toiling woman. God alone knows how I have supplicated with tears on my nightly couch, that I might be like her."

I threw myself at her feet, and, seizing her hand, bedewed it with a thousand tears. "Charlotte!" I exclaimed, "God's blessing and your mother's spirit are upon you." "Oh! that you had known her," she said, with a warm pressure of the hand. "She was worthy of being known to you." I thought I should have fainted: never had I received praise so flattering. She continued, "And yet she was doomed to die in the flower of her youth, when her youngest child was scarcely six months old. Her illness was but short, but she was calm and resigned; and it was only for her children, especially the youngest, that she felt unhappy. When her end drew nigh, she bade me bring them to her. I obeyed. The younger ones knew nothing of their approaching loss, while the elder ones were quite overcome with grief. They stood around the bed; and she raised her feeble hands to heaven, and prayed over them; then, kissing them in turn, she dismissed them, and said to me, 'Be you a mother to them.' I gave her my hand. 'You are promising much, my child,' she said: 'a mother's fondness and a mother's care! I have often witnessed, by your tears of gratitude, that you know what is a mother's tenderness: show it to your brothers and sisters and be dutiful and faithful to your father as a wife; you will be his comfort.' She inquired for him. He had retired to conceal his intolerable anguish, —he was heartbroken, 'Albert, you were in the room.' She heard someone moving, she inquired who it was, and desired you to approach. She surveyed us both with a look of composure and satisfaction, expressive of her conviction that we should be happy, —happy with one another." Albert fell upon her neck, and kissed her, and exclaimed, "We are so, and we shall be so!" Even Albert, generally so tranquil, had quite lost his composure; and I was excited beyond expression.

"And such a being," She continued, "was to leave us, Werther! Great God, must we thus part with everything we hold dear in this world? Nobody felt this more acutely than the children: they cried and lamented for a long time afterward, complaining that men had carried away their dear mamma."

Charlotte rose. It aroused me; but I continued sitting and held her hand. "Let us go," she said: "it grows late." She attempted to withdraw her hand: I held it still. "We shall see each other again," I exclaimed: "we shall recognize each other under every possible change! I am going," I continued, "going willingly; but should I say forever, perhaps I may not keep my word. Adieu, Charlotte; adieu, Albert. We shall meet again." "Yes: tomorrow, I think," she answered with a smile. Tomorrow! how I felt the word! Ah! she little thought when she drew her hand away from mine. They walked down the avenue. I stood gazing after them in the moonlight. I threw myself upon the ground, and wept; I then sprang up, and ran out upon the terrace, and saw, under the shade of the linden-trees, her white dress disappearing near the garden-gate. I stretched out my arms, and she vanished.

BOOK II

OCTOBER 20.

We arrived here yesterday. The ambassador is indisposed and will not go out for some days. If he were less peevish and morose, all would be well. I see but too plainly that Heaven has destined me to severe trials; but courage! a light heart may bear anything. A light heart! I smile to find such a word proceeding from my pen. A little more lightheartedness would render me the happiest being under the sun. But must I despair of my talents and faculties, whilst others of far inferior abilities parade before me with the utmost self-satisfaction? Gracious Providence, to whom I owe all my powers, why didst thou not withhold some of those blessings I possess, and substitute in their place a feeling of self-confidence and contentment?

But patience! all will yet be well; for I assure you, my dear friend, you were right: since I have been obliged to associate continually with other people, and observe what they do, and how they employ themselves, I have become far better satisfied with myself. For we are so constituted by nature, that we are ever prone to compare ourselves with others; and our happiness or misery depends very much on the objects and persons around us. On this account, nothing is more dangerous than solitude: there our imagination, always disposed to rise, taking a new flight on the wings of fancy, pictures to us a chain of beings of whom we seem the most inferior. All things appear greater than they really are, and all seem superior to us. This operation of the mind is quite natural: we so continually feel our own imperfections, and fancy we perceive in others the qualities we do not possess, attributing to them also all that we enjoy ourselves, that by this process we form the idea of a perfect, happy man, —a man, however, who only exists in our own imagination.

But when, in spite of weakness and disappointments, we set to work in earnest, and persevere steadily, we often find, that, though obliged continually to tack, we make more way than others who have the assistance of wind and tide; and, in truth, there can be no greater satisfaction than to keep pace with others or outstrip them in the race.

November 26.

I begin to find my situation here more tolerable, considering all circumstances. I find a great advantage in being much occupied; and the number of persons I meet, and their different pursuits, create a varied entertainment for me. I have formed the acquaintance of the Count C—and I esteem him more and more every day. He is a man of strong understanding and great discernment; but though he sees farther than other people, he is not on that account cold in his manner, but capable of inspiring and returning the warmest affection. He appeared interested in me on one occasion, when I had to transact some business with him. He perceived, at the first word, that we understood each other, and that he could converse with me in a different tone from what he used with others. I cannot sufficiently esteem his frank and open kindness to me. It is the greatest and most genuine of pleasures to observe a great mind in sympathy with our own.

DECEMBER 24.

As I anticipated, the ambassador occasions me infinite

annoyance. He is the most punctilious blockhead under heaven. He does everything step by step, with the trifling minuteness of an old woman; and he is a man whom it is impossible to please, because he is never pleased with himself. I like to do business regularly and cheerfully, and, when it is finished, to leave it. But he constantly returns my papers to me, saying, "They will do," but recommending me to look over them again, as "one may always improve by using a better word or a more appropriate particle." I then lose all patience and wish myself at the devils. Not a conjunction, not an adverb, must be omitted: he has a deadly antipathy to all those transpositions of which I am so fond; and, if the music of our periods is not tuned to the established, official key, he cannot comprehend our meaning. It is deplorable to be connected with such a fellow.

My acquaintance with the Count C—is the only compensation for such an evil. He told me frankly, the other day, that he was much displeased with the difficulties and delays of the ambassador; that people like him are obstacles, both to themselves and to others. "But," added he, "one must submit, like a traveller who has to ascend a mountain: if the mountain was not there, the road would be both shorter and pleasanter; but there it is, and he must get over it."

The old man perceives the count's partiality for me: this annoys him, and he seizes every opportunity to depreciate the count in my hearing. I naturally defend him and that only makes matters worse. Yesterday he made me indignant, for he also alluded to me. "The count," he said, "is a man of the world, and a good man of business: his style is good, and he writes with facility; but, like other geniuses, he has no solid learning." He looked at me with an expression that seemed to ask if I felt the blow. But it did not produce the desired effect: I despise a man who can think and act in such a manner. However, I made a stand, and answered with not a little warmth. The count, I said, was a man entitled to respect, alike for his character and his acquirements. I had never met a person whose mind was stored with more useful and extensive knowledge, —who had, in fact, mastered such an infinite variety of subjects, and who yet retained all his activity for the details of ordinary business. This was altogether beyond his comprehension; and I took my leave, lest my anger should be too highly excited by some new absurdity of his.

And you are to blame for all this, you who persuaded me to bend my neck to this yoke by preaching a life of activity to me. If the man who plants vegetables and carries his corn to town on market-days, is not more usefully employed than I am, then let me work ten years longer at the galleys to which I am now chained.

Oh, the brilliant wretchedness, the weariness, that one is doomed to witness among the silly people whom we meet in society here! The ambition of rank! How they watch, how they toil, to gain precedence! What poor and contemptible passions are displayed in their utter nakedness! We have a woman here, for example, who never ceases to entertain the company with accounts of her family and her estates. Any stranger would consider her a silly being, whose head was turned by her pretensions to rank and property; but she is in reality even more ridiculous, the daughter of a mere magistrate's clerk from this neighbourhood. I cannot understand how human beings can so debase themselves.

Every day I observe more and more the folly of judging of others by ourselves, and I have so much trouble with myself, and my own heart is in such constant agitation, that I am well content to let others pursue their own course, if they only allow me the same privilege.

What provokes me most is the unhappy extent to which distinctions of rank are carried. I know perfectly well how necessary are inequalities of condition and I am sensible of the advantages I myself derive therefrom; but I would not have these institutions prove a barrier to the small chance of happiness which I may enjoy on this earth.

I have lately become acquainted with a Miss B—, a very agreeable girl, who has retained her natural manners in the midst of artificial life. Our first conversation pleased us both equally; and, at taking leave, I requested permission to visit her. She consented in so obliging a manner, that I waited with impatience for the arrival of the happy moment. She is not a native of this place but resides here with her aunt. The countenance of the old lady is not prepossessing. I paid her much attention, addressing the greater part of my conversation to her; and, in less than half an hour, I discovered what her niece subsequently acknowledged to me, that her aged aunt, having but a small fortune, and a still smaller share of understanding, enjoys no satisfaction except in the pedigree of her ancestors, no protection save in her noble birth, and no enjoyment but in looking from her castle over the heads of the humble citizens. She was, no doubt, handsome in her youth, and in her early years probably trifled away her time in rendering many a poor youth the sport of her caprice: in her riper years she has submitted to the yoke of a veteran officer, who, in return for her person and her small independence, has spent with her what we may designate her age of brass. He is dead; and she is now a widow and deserted. She spends her iron age alone, and would not be approached, except for the loveliness of her niece.

JANUARY 8, 1772.

What beings are men, whose whole thoughts are occupied with form and ceremony, who for years together devote their mental and physical exertions to the task of advancing themselves but one step and endeavoring to occupy a higher place at the table. Not that such persons would otherwise want employment: on the contrary, they give themselves much trouble by neglecting important business for such petty trifles. Last week a question of precedence arose at a sledging-party, and all our amusement was spoiled.

The silly creatures cannot see that it is not place which constitutes real greatness, since the man who occupies the first place but seldom plays the principal part. How many kings are governed by their ministers—how many ministers by their secretaries? Who, in such cases, is really the chief? He, as it seems to me, who can see through the others, and possesses strength or skill enough to make their power or passions subservient to the execution of his own designs.

JANUARY 20.

I must write to you from this place, my dear Charlotte, from a small room in a country inn, where I have taken shelter from a severe storm. During my whole residence in that wretched place D—, where I lived amongst strangers, —strangers, indeed, to this heart, —I never at any time felt the smallest inclination to correspond with you; but in this cottage, in this retirement, in this solitude, with the snow and hail beating against my lattice-pane, you are my first thought. The instant I entered, your figure rose up before me, and the remembrance! O my Charlotte, the sacred, tender remembrance! Gracious Heaven! restore to me the happy moment of our first acquaintance.

Could you but see me, my dear Charlotte, in the whirl of dissipation, —how my senses are dried up, but my heart is at no time full. I enjoy no single moment of happiness: all is vain—nothing touches me. I stand, as it were, before the raree-show: I see the little puppets move, and I ask whether it is not an optical illusion. I am amused with these puppets, or, rather, I am myself one of them: but, when I sometimes grasp my neighbour's hand, I feel that it is not natural; and I withdraw mine with a shudder. In the evening I say I will enjoy the next morning's sunrise, and yet I remain in bed: in the day I promise to ramble by moonlight; and I, nevertheless, remain at home. I know not why I rise, nor why I go to sleep.

The leaven which animated my existence is gone: the charm which cheered me in the gloom of night, and aroused me from my morning slumbers, is forever fled.

I have found but one being here to interest me, a Miss B—. She resembles you, my dear Charlotte, if anyone can possibly resemble you. "Ah!" you will say, "he has learned how to pay fine compliments." And this is partly true. I have been very agreeable lately, as it was not in my power to be otherwise. I have, moreover, a deal of wit: and the ladies say that no one understands flattery better, or falsehoods you will add since one accomplishment invariably accompanies the other. But I must tell you of Miss B—. She has abundance of soul, which flashes from her deep blue eyes. Her rank is a torment to her and satisfies no one desire of her heart. She would gladly retire from this whirl of fashion, and we often picture to ourselves a life of undisturbed happiness in distant scenes of rural retirement: and then we speak of you, my dear Charlotte; for she knows you, and renders homage to your merits; but her homage is not exacted, but voluntary, she loves you, and delights to hear you made the subject of conversation.

Oh, that I were sitting at your feet in your favourite little room, with the dear children playing around us! If they became troublesome to you, I would tell them some appalling goblin story; and they would crowd round me with silent attention. The sun is setting in glory; his last rays are shining on the snow, which covers the face of the country: the storm is over, and I must return to my dungeon. Adieu! —Is Albert with you? and what is he to you? God forgive the question.

FEBRUARY 8.

For a week past we have had the most wretched weather: but this to me is a blessing; for, during my residence here, not a single fine day has beamed from the heavens but has been lost to me by the intrusion of somebody. During the severity of rain, sleet, frost, and storm, I congratulate myself that it cannot be worse indoors than abroad, nor worse abroad than it is within doors; and so, I become reconciled. When the sun rises bright in the morning, and promises a glorious day, I never omit to exclaim, "There, now, they have another blessing from Heaven, which they will be sure to destroy: they spoil everything, —health, fame, happiness, amusement; and they do this generally through folly, ignorance, or imbecility, and always, according to their own account, with the best intentions!" I could often beseech them, on my bended knees, to be less resolved upon their own destruction.

FEBRUARY 17.

I fear that my ambassador and I shall not continue much longer together. He is really growing past endurance. He transacts his business in so ridiculous a manner, that I am often compelled to contradict him, and do things my own way; and then, of course, he thinks them very ill done. He complained of me lately on this account at court; and the minister gave me a reprimand, —a gentle one it is true, but still a reprimand. In consequence of this, I was about to tender my resignation, when I received a letter, to which I submitted with great respect, on account of the high, noble, and generous spirit which dictated it. He endeavoured to soothe my excessive sensibility, paid a tribute to my extreme ideas of duty, of good example, and of perseverance in business, as the fruit of my youthful ardour, an impulse which he did not seek to destroy, but only to moderate, that it might have proper play and be productive of good. So now I am at rest for another week, and no longer at variance with myself. Content and peace of mind are valuable things: I could wish, my dear friend, that these precious jewels were less transitory.

FEBRUARY 20.

God bless you, my dear friends, and may he grant you that

happiness which he denies to me!

I thank you, Albert, for having deceived me. I waited for the news that your wedding-day was fixed; and I intended on that day, with solemnity, to take down Charlotte's profile from the wall, and to bury it with some other papers I possess. You are now united, and her picture still remains here. Well, let it remain! Why should it not? I know that I am still one of your society, that I still occupy a place uninjured in Charlotte's heart, that I hold the second place therein; and I intend to keep it. Oh, I should become mad if she could forget! Albert, that thought is hell! Farewell, Albert farewell, angel of heaven farewell, Charlotte!

MARCH 15.

I have just had a sad adventure, which will drive me away from here. I lose all patience! —Death!—It is not to be remedied; and you alone are to blame, for you urged and impelled me to fill a post for which I was by no means suited. Now I have reason to be satisfied, and so have you! But that you may not again attribute this fatality to my impetuous temper, I send you, my dear sir, a plain and simple narration of the affair, as a mere chronicler of facts would describe it.

The Count of O—likes and distinguishes me. It is well known, and I have mentioned this to you a hundred times. Yesterday I dined with him. It is the day on which the nobility are accustomed to assemble at his house in the evening. I never once thought of the assembly, nor that we subalterns did not belong to such society. Well, I dined with the count; and, after dinner, we adjourned to the large hall. We walked up and down together: and I conversed with him, and with Colonel B—, who joined us; and in this manner the hour for the assembly approached. God knows, I was thinking of nothing, when who should enter but the honourable Lady accompanied by her noble husband and their silly, scheming daughter, with her small waist and flat neck; and, with disdainful looks and a haughty air they passed me by. As I heartily detest the whole race, I determined upon going away; and only waited till the count had disengaged himself from their impertinent prattle, to take leave, when the agreeable Miss B—came in. As I never meet her without experiencing a heartfelt pleasure, I stayed and talked to her, leaning over the back of her chair, and did not perceive, till after some time, that she seemed a little confused, and ceased to answer me with her usual ease of manner. I was struck with it. "Heavens!" I said to myself, "can she, too, be like the rest?" I felt annoyed, and was about to withdraw; but I remained, notwithstanding, forming excuses for her conduct, fancying she did not mean it, and still hoping to receive some friendly recognition. The rest of the company now arrived. There was the Baron F—, in an entire suit that dated from the coronation of Francis I.; the Chancellor N—, with his deaf wife; the shabbily-dressed I—, whose old-fashioned coat bore evidence of modern repairs: this crowned the whole. I conversed with some of my acquaintances, but they answered me laconically. I was engaged in observing Miss B—, and did not notice that the women were whispering at the end of the room, that the murmur extended by degrees to the men, that Madame S—addressed the count with much warmth (this was all related to me subsequently by Miss B—); till at length the count came up to me, and took me to the window. "You know our ridiculous customs," he said. "I perceive the company is rather displeased at your being here. I would not on any account—" "I beg your excellency's pardon!" I exclaimed. "I ought to have thought of this before, but I know you will forgive this little inattention. I was going," I added, "some time ago, but my evil genius detained me." And I smiled and bowed, to take my leave. He shook me by the hand, in a manner which expressed everything. I hastened at once from the illustrious assembly, sprang into a carriage, and drove to M—. I contemplated the setting sun from the top of the hill, and read that beautiful passage in Homer, where Ulysses is entertained by the hospitable herdsmen. This was indeed delightful.

I returned home to supper in the evening. But few persons were assembled in the room. They had turned up a corner of the tablecloth and were playing at dice. The good-natured A—came in. He laid down his hat when he saw me, approached me, and said in a low tone, "You have met with a disagreeable adventure." "I!" I exclaimed. "The count obliged you to withdraw from the assembly!" "Deuce take the assembly!" said I. "I was very glad to be gone." "I am delighted," he added, "that you take it so lightly. I am only sorry that it is already so much spoken of." The circumstance then began to pain me. I fancied that everyone who sat down, and even looked at me, was thinking of this incident; and my heart became embittered.

And now I could plunge a dagger into my bosom, when I hear myself everywhere pitied, and observe the triumph of my enemies, who say that this is always the case with vain persons, whose heads are turned with conceit, who affect to despise forms and such petty, idle nonsense.

Say what you will of fortitude but show me the man who can patiently endure the laughter of fools, when they have obtained an advantage over him. 'Tis only when their nonsense is without foundation that one can suffer it without complaint.

March 16.

Everything conspires against me. I met Miss B—walking to-day. I could not help joining her; and, when we were at a little distance from her companions, I expressed my sense of her altered manner toward me. "O Werther!" she said, in a tone of emotion, "you, who know my heart, how could you so ill interpret my distress? What did I not suffer for you, from the moment you entered the room! I foresaw it all, a hundred times was I on the point of mentioning it to you. I knew that the S——s and T——s, with their husbands, would quit the room, rather than remain in your company. I knew that the count would not break with them: and now so much is said about it." "How!" I exclaimed and endeavoured to conceal my emotion; for all that Adelin had mentioned to me yesterday recurred to me painfully at that moment. "Oh, how much it has already cost me!" said this amiable girl, while her eyes filled with tears. I could scarcely contain myself and was ready to throw myself at her feet. "Explain yourself!" I cried. Tears flowed down her cheeks. I became quite frantic. She wiped them away, without attempting to conceal them. "You know my aunt," she continued; "she was present: and in what light does she consider the affair! Last night, and this morning, Werther, I was compelled to listen to a lecture upon my acquaintance with you. I have been obliged to hear you condemned and depreciated; and I could not—I dared not—say much in your defence."

Every word she uttered was a dagger to my heart. She did not feel what a mercy it would have been to conceal everything from me. She told me, in addition, all the impertinence that would be further circulated, and how the malicious would triumph; how they would rejoice over the punishment of my pride, over my humiliation for that want of esteem for others with which I had often been reproached. To hear all this, Wilhelm, uttered by her in a voice of sincerest sympathy, awakened all my passions; and I am still in a state of extreme excitement. I wish I could find a man to jeer me about this event. I would sacrifice him to my resentment. The sight of his blood might possibly be a relief to my fury. A hundred times have I seized a dagger, to give ease to this oppressed heart. Naturalists tell of a noble race of horses that instinctively open a vein with their teeth, when heated and exhausted by a long course, in order to breathe more freely. I am often tempted to open a vein, to procure for myself everlasting liberty.

MARCH 24.

I have tendered my resignation to the court. I hope it will be accepted, and you will forgive me for not having previously consulted you. It is necessary I should leave this place. I know all you will urge me to stay, and therefore I beg you will soften this news to my mother. I am unable to do anything for myself: how, then, should I be competent to assist others? It will afflict her that I should have interrupted that career which would have made me first a privy councillor and then minister, and that I should look behind me, in place of advancing. Argue as you will, combine all the reasons which should have induced me to remain, I am going that is sufficient. But that you may not be ignorant of my destination, I may mention that the prince of—is here. He is much pleased with my company; and, having heard of my intention to resign, he has invited me to his country house, to pass the spring months with him. I shall be left completely my own master; and, as we agree on all subjects but one, I shall try my fortune, and accompany him.

APRIL 19.

Thanks for both your letters. I delayed my reply, and withheld this letter, till I should obtain an answer from the court. I feared my mother might apply to the minister to defeat my purpose. But my request is granted, my resignation is accepted. I shall not recount with what reluctance it was accorded, nor relate what the minister has written: you would only renew your lamentations. The crown prince has sent me a present of five and twenty ducats; and, indeed, such goodness has affected me to tears. For this reason, I shall not require from my mother the money for which I lately applied.

MAY 5.

I leave this place to-morrow; and, as my native place is only six miles from the high road, I intend to visit it once more, and recall the happy dreams of my childhood. I shall enter at the same gate through which I came with my mother, when, after my father's death, she left that delightful retreat to immure herself in your melancholy town. Adieu, my dear friend: you shall hear of my future career.

MAY 9.

I have paid my visit to my native place with all the devotion of a pilgrim and have experienced many unexpected emotions. Near the great elm tree, which is a quarter of a league from the village, I got out of the carriage, and sent it on before, that alone, and on foot, I might enjoy vividly and heartily all the pleasure of my recollections. I stood there under that same elm which was formerly the term and object of my walks. How things have since changed! Then, in happy ignorance, I sighed for a world I did not know, where I hoped to find every pleasure and enjoyment which my heart could desire; and now, on my return from that wide world, O my friend, how many disappointed hopes and unsuccessful plans have I brought back!

As I contemplated the mountains which lay stretched out before me, I thought how often they had been the object of my dearest desires. Here used I to sit for hours together with my eyes bent upon them, ardently longing to wander in the shade of those woods, to lose myself in those valleys, which form so delightful an object in the distance. With what reluctance did I leave this charming spot; when my hour of recreation was over, and my leave of absence expired! I drew near to the village: all the well-known old summerhouses and gardens were recognized again; I disliked the new ones, and all other alterations which had taken place. I entered the village, and all my former feelings returned. I cannot, my dear friend, enter into details, charming as were my sensations: they would be dull in the narration. I had intended to lodge in the marketplace, near our old house. As soon as I entered, I perceived that the schoolroom, where our childhood had been taught by that good old woman, was converted into a shop. I called to mind the sorrow, the heaviness, the tears, and oppression of heart, which I experienced in that confinement. Every step produced some particular impression. A pilgrim in the Holy Land does not meet so many spots pregnant with tender recollections, and his soul is hardly moved with greater devotion. One incident will serve for illustration. I followed the course of a stream to a farm, formerly a delightful walk of mine, and paused at the spot, where, when boys, we used to amuse ourselves making ducks and drakes upon the water. I recollected so well how I used formerly to watch the course of that same stream, following it with inquiring eagerness, forming romantic ideas of the countries it was to pass through; but my imagination was soon exhausted: while the water continued flowing farther and farther on, till my fancy became bewildered by the contemplation of an invisible distance. Exactly such, my dear friend, so happy and so confined, were the thoughts of our good ancestors. Their feelings and their poetry were fresh as childhood. And, when Ulysses talks of the immeasurable sea and boundless earth, his epithets are true, natural, deeply felt, and mysterious. Of what importance is it that I have learned, with every schoolboy, that the world is round? Man needs but little earth for enjoyment, and still less for his final repose.

I am at present with the prince at his hunting lodge. He is a man with whom one can live happily. He is honest and unaffected. There are, however, some strange characters about him, whom I cannot at all understand. They do not seem vicious, and yet they do not carry the appearance of thoroughly honest men. Sometimes I am disposed to believe them honest, and yet I cannot persuade myself to confide in them. It grieves me to hear the prince occasionally talk of things which he has only read or heard of, and always with the same view in which they have been represented by others.

He values my understanding and talents more highly than my heart, but I am proud of the latter only. It is the sole source of everything of our strength, happiness, and misery. All the knowledge I possess everyone else can acquire, but my heart is exclusively my own.

MAY 25.

I have had a plan in my head of which I did not intend to speak to you until it was accomplished: now that it has failed, I may as well mention it. I wished to enter the army and had long been desirous of taking the step. This, indeed, was the chief reason for my coming here with the prince, as he is a general in the service. I communicated my design to him during one of our walks together. He disapproved of it, and it would have been actual madness not to have listened to his reasons.

JUNE 11.

Say what you will, I can remain here no longer. Why should I remain? Time hangs heavy upon my hands. The prince is as gracious to me as anyone could be, and yet I am not at my ease. There is, indeed, nothing in common between us. He is a man of understanding, but quite of the ordinary kind. His conversation affords me no more amusement than I should derive from the perusal of a well-written book. I shall remain here a week longer, and then start again on my travels. My drawings are the best things I have done since I came here. The prince has a taste for the arts and would improve if his mind were not fettered by cold rules and mere technical ideas. I often lose patience, when, with a glowing imagination, I am giving expression to art and nature, he interferes with learned suggestions, and uses at random the technical phraseology of artists.

JULY 16.

Once more I am a wanderer, a pilgrim, through the world. But what else are you!

JULY 18.

Whither am I going? I will tell you in confidence. I am obliged to continue a fortnight longer here, and then I think it would be better for me to visit the mines in—. But I am only deluding myself thus. The fact is, I wish to be near Charlotte again, that is all. I smile at the suggestions of my heart and obey its dictates.

JULY 29.

No, no! it is yet well all is well! I her husband! O God, who gave me being, if thou hadst destined this happiness for me, my whole life would have been one continual thanksgiving! But I will not murmur—forgive these tears, forgive these fruitless wishes. She—my wife! Oh, the very thought of folding that dearest of Heaven's creatures in my arms! Dear Wilhelm, my whole frame feels convulsed when I see Albert put his arms around her slender waist!

And shall I avow it? Why should I not, Wilhelm? She would have been happier with me than with him. Albert is not the man to satisfy the wishes of such a heart. He wants a certain sensibility; he wants—in short, their hearts do not beat in unison. How often, my dear friend, I'm reading a passage from some interesting book, when my heart and Charlotte's seemed to meet, and in a hundred other instances when our sentiments were unfolded by the story of some fictitious character, have I felt that we were made for each other! But, dear Wilhelm, he loves her with his whole soul; and what does not such a love deserve?

I have been interrupted by an insufferable visit. I have dried my tears and composed my thoughts. Adieu, my best friend!

AUGUST 4.

I am not alone unfortunate. All men are disappointed in their hopes and deceived in their expectations. I have paid a visit to my good old woman under the lime-trees. The eldest boy ran out to meet me: his exclamation of joy brought out his mother, but she had a very melancholy look. Her first word was, "Alas! dear sir, my little John is dead."

He was the youngest of her children. I was silent. "And my husband has returned from Switzerland without any money; and, if some kind people had not assisted him, he must have begged his way home. He was taken ill with fever on his journey." I could answer nothing but made the little one a present. She invited me to take some fruit: I complied and left the place with a sorrowful heart.

AUGUST 21.

My sensations are constantly changing. Sometimes a happy prospect opens before me; but alas! it is only for a moment; and then, when I am lost in reverie, I cannot help saying to myself, "If Albert were to die?—Yes, she would become—and I should be"—and so I pursue a chimera, till it leads me to the edge of a precipice at which I shudder.

When I pass through the same gate and walk along the same road which first conducted me to Charlotte, my heart sinks within me at the change that has since taken place. All, all, is altered! No sentiment, no pulsation of my heart, is the same. My sensations are such as would occur to some departed prince whose spirit should return to visit the superb palace which he had built in happy times, adorned with costly magnificence, and left to a beloved son, but whose glory he should find departed, and its halls deserted and in ruins.

SEPTEMBER 3.

I sometimes cannot understand how she can love another, how she dares love another, when I love nothing in this world so completely, so devotedly, as I love her, when I know only her, and have no other possession.

SEPTEMBER 4.

It is even so! As nature puts on her autumn tints it becomes autumn with me and around me. My leaves are sere and yellow, and the neighbouring trees are divested of their foliage. Do you remember my writing to you about a peasant boy shortly after my arrival here? I have just made inquiries about him in Walheim. They say he has been dismissed from his service and is now avoided by everyone. I met him yesterday on the road, going to a neighbouring village. I spoke to him, and he told me his story. It interested me exceedingly, as you will easily understand when I repeat it to you. But why should I trouble you? Why should I not reserve all my sorrow for myself? Why should I continue to give you occasion to pity and blame me? But no matter: this also is part of my destiny.

At first the peasant lad answered my inquiries with a sort of subdued melancholy, which seemed to me the mark of a timid disposition; but, as we grew to understand each other, he spoke with less reserve, and openly confessed his faults, and lamented his misfortune. I wish, my dear friend, I could give proper expression to his language. He told me with a sort of pleasurable recollection, that, after my departure, his passion for his mistress increased daily, until at last he neither knew what he did nor what he said, nor what was to become of him. He could neither eat nor drink nor sleep, he felt a sense of suffocation; he disobeyed all orders and forgot all commands involuntarily; he seemed as if pursued by an evil spirit, till one day, knowing that his mistress had gone to an upper chamber, he had followed, or, rather, been drawn after her. As she proved deaf to his entreaties, he had recourse to violence. He knows not what happened; but he called God to witness that his intentions to her were honourable, and that he desired nothing more sincerely than that they should marry and pass their lives together. When he had come to this point, he began to hesitate, as if there was something which he had not courage to utter, till at length he acknowledged with some confusion certain little confidences she had encouraged, and liberties she had allowed. He broke off two or three times in his narration and assured me most earnestly that he had no wish to make her bad, as he termed it, for he loved her still as sincerely as ever; that the tale had never before escaped his lips and was only now told to convince me that he was not utterly lost and abandoned. And here, my dear friend, I must commence the old song which you know I utter eternally. If I could only represent the man as he stood, and stands now before me, could I only give his true expressions, you would feel compelled to sympathize in his fate. But enough: you, who know my misfortune and my disposition, can easily comprehend the attraction which draws me toward every unfortunate being, but particularly toward him whose story I have recounted.

On perusing this letter, a second time, I find I have omitted the conclusion of my tale; but it is easily supplied. She became reserved toward him, at the instigation of her brother who had long hated him, and desired his expulsion from the house, fearing that his sister's second marriage might deprive his children of the handsome fortune they expected from her, as she is childless. He was dismissed at length; and the whole affair occasioned so much scandal, that the mistress dared not take him back, even if she had wished it. She has since hired another servant, with whom, they say, her brother is equally displeased, and whom she is likely to marry; but my informant assures me that he himself is determined not to survive such a catastrophe.

This story is neither exaggerated nor embellished: indeed, I have weakened and impaired it in the narration, by the necessity of using the more refined expressions of society.

This love, then, this constancy, this passion, is no poetical fiction. It is actual, and dwells in its greatest purity amongst that class of mankind whom we term rude, uneducated. We are the educated, not the perverted. But read this story with attention, I implore you. I am tranquil today, for I have been employed upon this narration: you see by my writing that I am not so agitated as usual. I read and re-read this tale, Wilhelm: it is the history of your friend! My fortune has been and will be similar; and I am neither half so brave nor half so determined as the poor wretch with whom I hesitate to compare myself.

SEPTEMBER 5.

Charlotte had written a letter to her husband in the country, where he was detained by business. It commenced, "My dearest love, return as soon as possible: I await you with a thousand raptures." A friend who arrived, brought word, that, for certain reasons, he could not return immediately. Charlotte's letter was not forwarded, and the same evening it fell into my hands. I read it and smiled. She asked the reason. "What a heavenly treasure is imagination:" I exclaimed; "I fancied for a moment that this was written to me." She paused and seemed displeased. I was silent.

SEPTEMBER 6.

It cost me much to part with the blue coat which I wore the first time I danced with Charlotte. But I could not possibly wear it any longer. But I have ordered a new one, precisely similar, even to the collar and sleeves, as well as new waistcoat and pantaloons.

But it does not produce the same effect upon me. I don't know how it is, but I hope in time I shall like it better.

SEPTEMBER 12.

She has been absent for some days. She went to meet Albert. Today I visited her: she rose to receive me, and I kissed her hand most tenderly.

A canary at the moment flew from a mirror and settled upon her shoulder. "Here is a new friend," she observed, while she made him perch upon her hand: "he is a present for the children. What a dear he is! Look at him! When I feed him, he flutters with his wings, and pecks so nicely. He kisses me, too, only look!"

She held the bird to her mouth; and he pressed her sweet lips with so much fervour that he seemed to feel the excess of bliss which he enjoyed.

"He shall kiss you too," she added; and then she held the bird toward me. His little beak moved from her mouth to mine, and the delightful sensation seemed like the forerunner of the sweetest bliss.

"A kiss," I observed, "does not seem to satisfy him: he wishes for food and seems disappointed by these unsatisfactory endearments."

"But he eats out of my mouth," she continued, and extended her lips to him containing seed; and she smiled with all the charm of a being who has allowed an innocent participation of her love.

I turned my face away. She should not act thus. She ought not to excite my imagination with such displays of heavenly innocence and happiness, nor awaken my heart from its slumbers, in which it dreams of the worthlessness of life! And why not? Because she knows how much I love her.

SEPTEMBER 15.

It makes me wretched, Wilhelm, to think that there should be men incapable of appreciating the few things which possess a real value in life. You remember the walnut trees at S—, under which I used to sit with Charlotte, during my visits to the worthy old vicar. Those glorious trees, the very sight of which has so often filled my heart with joy, how they adorned and refreshed the parsonage yard, with their wide-extended branches! and how pleasing was our remembrance of the good old pastor, by whose hands they were planted so many years ago: The schoolmaster has frequently mentioned his name. He had it from his grandfather. He must have been a most excellent man; and, under the shade of those old trees, his memory was ever venerated by me. The schoolmaster informed us yesterday, with tears in his eyes, that those trees had been felled. Yes, cut to the ground! I could, in my wrath, have slain the monster who struck the first stroke. And I must endure this! —I, who, if I had had two such trees in my own court, and one had died from old age, should have wept with real affliction. But there is some comfort left, such a thing is sentiment, the whole village murmurs at the misfortune; and I hope the vicar's wife will soon find, by the cessation of the villagers' presents, how much she has wounded the feelings of the neighborhhood. It was she who did it, the wife of the present incumbent (our good old man is dead), a tall, sickly creature who is so far right to disregard the world, as the world totally disregards her. The silly being affects to be learned, pretends to examine the canonical books, lends her aid toward the new-fashioned reformation of Christendom, moral and critical, and shrugs up her shoulders at the mention of Lavater's enthusiasm. Her health is destroyed, on account of which she is prevented from having any enjoyment here below. Only such a creature could have cut down my walnut trees! I can never pardon it. Hear her reasons. The falling leaves made the court wet and dirty; the branches obstructed the light; boys threw stones at the nuts when they were ripe, and the noise affected her nerves; and disturbed her profound meditations, when she was weighing the difficulties of Kennicot, Semler and Michaelis. Finding that all the parish, particularly the old people, were displeased, I asked "why they allowed it?" "Ah, sir!" they replied, "when the steward orders, what can we poor peasants do?" But one thing has happened well. The steward and the vicar (who, for once, thought to reap some advantage from the caprices of his wife) intended to divide the trees between them. The revenue-office, being informed of it, revived an old claim to the ground where the trees had stood, and sold them to the best bidder. There they still lie on the ground. If I were the sovereign, I should know how to deal with them all, vicar, steward, and revenue-office. Sovereign, did I say? I should, in that case, care little about the trees that grew in the country.

OCTOBER 10.

Only to gaze upon her dark eyes is to me a source of happiness! And what grieves me, is, that Albert does not seem so happy as he—hoped to be—as I should have been—if—I am no friend to these pauses, but here I cannot express it otherwise; and probably I am explicit enough.

OCTOBER 12.

Ossian has superseded Homer in my heart. To what a world does the illustrious bard carry me! To wander over pathless wilds, surrounded by impetuous whirlwinds, where, by the feeble light of the moon, we see the spirits of our ancestors; to hear from the mountain-tops, mid the roar of torrents, their plaintive sounds issuing from deep caverns, and the sorrowful lamentations of a maiden who sighs and expires on the mossy tomb of the warrior by whom she was adored. I meet this bard with silver hair; he wanders in the valley; he seeks the footsteps of his fathers and alas! he finds only their tombs. Then, contemplating the pale moon, as she sinks beneath the waves of the rolling sea, the memory of bygone days strikes the mind of the hero, days when approaching danger invigorated the brave, and the moon shone upon his bark laden with spoils, and returning in triumph. When I read in his countenance deep sorrow, when I see his dying glory sink exhausted into the grave, as he inhales new and heart-thrilling delight from his approaching union with his beloved, and he casts a look on the cold earth and the tall grass which is so soon to cover him, and then exclaims, "The traveller will come,—he will come who has seen my beauty, and he will ask, 'Where is the bard, where is the illustrious son of Fingal?' He will walk over my tomb and will seek me in vain!" Then, O my friend, I could instantly, like a true and noble knight, draw my sword, and deliver my prince from the long and painful languor of a living death, and dismiss my own soul to follow the demigod whom my hand had set free!

OCTOBER 19.

Alas! the void the fearful void, which I feel in my bosom! Sometimes I think, if I could only once but once, press her to my heart, this dreadful void would be filled.

OCTOBER 26.

Yes, I feel certain, Wilhelm, and every day I become more certain, that the existence of any being whatever is of very little consequence. A friend of Charlotte's called to see her just now. I withdrew into a neighbouring apartment, and took up a book; but, finding I could not read, I sat down to write. I heard them converse in an undertone: they spoke upon indifferent topics and retailed the news of the town. One was going to be married; another was ill, very ill, she had a dry cough, her face was growing thinner daily, and she had occasional fits. "N—is very unwell too," said Charlotte. "His limbs begin to swell already," answered the other; and my lively imagination carried me at once to the beds of the infirm. There I see them struggling against death, with all the agonies of pain and horror; and these women, Wilhelm, talk of all this with as much indifference as one would mention the death of a stranger. And when I look around the apartment where I now am—when I see Charlotte's apparel lying before me, and Albert's writings, and all those articles of furniture which are so familiar to me, even to the very inkstand which I am using, —when I think what I am to this family—everything. My friends esteem me; I often contribute to their happiness, and my heart seems as if it could not beat without them; and yet—-if I were to die, if I were to be summoned from the midst of this circle, would they feel—or how long would they feel the void which my loss would make in their existence? How long! Yes, such is the frailty of man, that even there, where he has the greatest consciousness of his own being, where he makes the strongest and most forcible impression, even in the memory, in the heart, of his beloved, there also he must perish, —vanish, —and that quickly.

OCTOBER 27.

I could tear open my bosom with vexation to think how little we are capable of influencing the feelings of each other. No one can communicate to me those sensations of love, joy, rapture, and delight which I do not naturally possess; and, though my heart may glow with the liveliest affection, I cannot make the happiness of one in whom the same warmth is not inherent.

OCTOBER 27: Evening.

I possess so much, but my love for her absorbs it all. I possess so much, but without her I have nothing.

OCTOBER 30.

One hundred times have I been on the point of embracing her. Heavens! what a torment it is to see so much loveliness passing and repassing before us, and yet not dare to lay hold of it! And laying hold is the most natural of human instincts. Do not children touch everything they see? And I!

NOVEMBER 3.

Witness, Heaven, how often I lie down in my bed with a wish, and even a hope, that I may never awaken again. And in the morning, when I open my eyes, I behold the sun once more, and am wretched. If I were whimsical, I might blame the weather, or an acquaintance, or some personal disappointment, for my discontented mind; and then this insupportable load of trouble would not rest entirely upon myself. But alas! I feel it too sadly. I am alone the cause of my own woe, am I not? Truly, my own bosom contains the source of all my sorrow, as it previously contained the source of all my pleasure. Am I not the same being who once enjoyed an excess of happiness, who, at every step, saw paradise open before him, and whose heart was ever expanded toward the whole world? And this heart is now dead, no sentiment can revive it; my eyes are dry;

and my senses, no more refreshed by the influence of soft tears, wither and consume my brain. I suffer much, for I have lost the only charm of life: that active, sacred power which created worlds around me, —it is no more. When I look from my window at the distant hills, and behold the morning sun breaking through the mists, and illuminating the country around, which is still wrapped in silence, whilst the soft stream winds gently through the willows, which have shed their leaves; when glorious nature displays all her beauties before me, and her wondrous prospects are ineffectual to extract one tear of joy from my withered heart, I feel that in such a moment I stand like a reprobate before heaven, hardened, insensible, and unmoved. Oftentimes do I then bend my knee to the earth, and implore God for the blessing of tears, as the desponding labourer in some scorching climate prays for the dews of heaven to moisten his parched corn.

But I feel that God does not grant sunshine or rain to our importunate entreaties. And oh, those bygone days, whose memory now torments me! why were they so fortunate? Because I then waited with patience for the blessings of the Eternal and received his gifts with the grateful feelings of a thankful heart.

NOVEMBER 8.

Charlotte has reproved me for my excesses, with so much tenderness and goodness! I have lately been in the habit of drinking more wine than heretofore. "Don't do it," she said. "Think of Charlotte!" "Think of you!" I answered, "need you bid me do so? Think of you—I do not think of you: you are ever before my soul! This very morning, I sat on the spot where, a few days ago, you descended from the carriage, and—" She immediately changed the subject to prevent me from pursuing it farther. My dear friend, my energies are all prostrated: she can do with me what she pleases.

NOVEMBER 15.

I thank you, Wilhelm, for your cordial sympathy, for your excellent advice; and I implore you to be quiet. Leave me to my sufferings. In spite of my wretchedness, I have still strength enough for endurance. I revere religion—you know I do. I feel that it can impart strength to the feeble and comfort to the afflicted, but does it affect all men equally? Consider this vast universe: you will see thousands for whom it has never existed, thousands for whom it will never exist, whether it be preached to them, or not; and must it, then, necessarily exist for me? Does not the Son of God himself say that they are his whom the Father has given to him? Have I been given to him? What if the father will retain me for himself, as my heart sometimes suggests? I pray you, do not misinterpret this. Do not extract derision from my harmless words. I pour out my whole soul before you. Silence were otherwise preferable to me, but I need not shrink from a subject of which few know more than I do myself. What is the destiny of man, but to fill up the measure of his sufferings, and to drink his allotted cup of bitterness? And if

that same cup proved bitter to the God of heaven, under a human form, why should I affect a foolish pride, and call it sweet? Why should I be ashamed of shrinking at that fearful moment, when my whole being will tremble between existence and annihilation, when a remembrance of the past, like a flash of lightning, will illuminate the dark gulf of futurity, when everything shall dissolve around me, and the whole world vanish away? Is not this the voice of a creature oppressed beyond all resource, self-deficient, about to plunge into inevitable destruction, and groaning deeply at its inadequate strength, "My God! my God! why hast thou forsaken me?" And should I feel ashamed to utter the same expression? Should I not shudder at a prospect which had its fears, even for him who folds up the heavens like a garment?

NOVEMBER 21.

She does not feel, she does not know, that she is preparing a poison which will destroy us both; and I drink deeply of the draught which is to prove my destruction. What mean those looks of kindness with which she often—often? no, not often, but sometimes, regards me, that complacency with which she hears the involuntary sentiments which frequently escape me, and the tender pity for my sufferings which appears in her countenance?

Yesterday, when I took leave she seized me by the hand, and said, "Adieu, dear Werther." Dear Werther! It was the first time she ever called me dear: the sound sunk deep into my heart. I have repeated it a hundred times; and last night, on going to bed, and talking to myself of various things, I suddenly said, "Good night, dear Werther!" and then could not but laugh at myself.

NOVEMBER 22

I cannot pray, "Leave her to me!" and yet she often seems to belong to me. I cannot pray, "Give her to me!" for she is another's. In this way I affect mirth over my troubles; and, if I had time, I could compose a whole litany of antitheses.

NOVEMBER 24.

She is sensible of my sufferings. This morning her look pierced my very soul. I found her alone and she was silent: she steadfastly surveyed me. I no longer saw in her face the charms of beauty or the fire of genius: these had disappeared. But I was affected by an expression much more touching, a look of the deepest sympathy and of the softest pity. Why was I afraid to throw myself at her feet? Why did I not dare to take her in my arms, and answer her by a thousand kisses? She had recourse to her piano for relief, and in a low and sweet voice accompanied the music with delicious sounds. Her lips never appeared so lovely: they seemed but just to open, that they might imbibe the sweet tones which were issued from the instrument and return the heavenly vibration from her lovely mouth. Oh! who can express my sensations? I was quite overcome, and, bending down, pronounced this vow: "Beautiful lips, which the angels guard, never will I seek to profane your purity with a kiss." And yet, my friend, oh, I wish—but my heart is darkened by doubt and indecision—could I but taste felicity, and then die to expiate the sin! What sin?

NOVEMBER 26.

Oftentimes I say to myself, "Thou alone art wretched: all other mortals are happy, none are distressed like thee!" Then I read a passage in an ancient poet, and I seem to understand my own heart. I have so much to endure! Have men before me ever been so wretched?

NOVEMBER 30.

I shall never be myself again! Wherever I go, some fatality occurs to distract me. Even today alas—for our destiny! alas for human nature!

About dinnertime I went to walk by the riverside, for I had no appetite. Everything around seemed gloomy: a cold and damp easterly wind blew from the mountains, and black, heavy clouds spread over the plain. I observed at a distance a man in a tattered coat: he was wandering among the rocks and seemed to be looking for plants. When I approached, he turned round at the noise; and I saw that he had an interesting countenance in which a settled melancholy, strongly marked by benevolence, formed the principal feature. His long black hair was divided and flowed over his shoulders. As his garb betokened a person of the lower order, I thought he would not take it ill if I inquired about his business; and I therefore asked what he was seeking. He replied, with a deep sigh, that he was looking for flowers, and could find none. "But it is not the season," I observed, with a smile. "Oh, there are so many flowers!" he answered, as he came nearer to me. "In my garden there are roses and honeysuckles of two sorts: one sort was given to me by my father! they grow as plentifully as weeds; I have been looking for them these two days and cannot find them. There are flowers out there, yellow, blue, and red; and that centaury has a very pretty blossom: but I can find none of them." I observed his peculiarity, and therefore asked him, with an air of indifference, what he intended to do with his flowers. A strange smile overspread his countenance. Holding his finger to his mouth, he expressed a hope that I would not betray him; and he then informed me that he had promised to gather a nosegay for his mistress. "That is right," said I. "Oh!" he replied, "she possesses many other things as well: she is very rich." "And yet," I continued, "she likes your nosegays." "Oh, she has jewels and crowns!" he exclaimed. I asked who she was. "If the states-general would but pay me," he added, "I should be quite another man. Alas! there was a time when I was so happy; but that is past, and I am now—" He raised his swimming eyes to heaven. "And you were happy once?" I observed. "Ah, would I were so still!" was his reply. "I was then as gay and contented as a man can be." An old woman, who was coming toward us, now called out, "Henry, Henry! where are you? We have been looking for you everywhere: come to dinner." "Is he your son?" I inquired, as I went toward her. "Yes," she said: "he is my poor, unfortunate son. The Lord has sent me a heavy affliction." I asked whether he had been long in this state. She answered, "He has been as calm as he is at present for about six months. I thank Heaven that he has so far recovered: he was for one whole year quite raving and chained down in a madhouse. Now he injures no one but talks of nothing else than kings and queens. He used to be a very good, quiet youth, and helped to maintain me; he wrote a very fine hand; but all at once he became melancholy, was seized with a violent fever, grew distracted, and is now as you see. If I were only to tell you, sir—" I interrupted her by asking what period it was in which he boasted of having been so happy. "Poor boy!" she exclaimed, with a smile of compassion, "he means the time when he was completely deranged, a time he never ceases to regret, when he was in the madhouse, and unconscious of everything." I was thunderstruck: I placed a piece of money in her hand and hastened away.

"You were happy!" I exclaimed, as I returned quickly to the town, "'as gay and contented as a man can be!'" God of heaven! and is this the destiny of man? Is he only happy before he has acquired his reason, or after he has lost it? Unfortunate being! And yet I envy your fate: I envy the delusion to which you are a victim. You go forth with joy to gather flowers for your princess, —in winter, —and grieve when you can find none, and cannot understand why they do not grow. But I wander forth without joy, without hope, without design; and I return as I came. You fancy what a man you would be if the state's general paid you. Happy mortal, who can ascribe your wretchedness to an earthly cause! You do not know, you do not feel, that in your own distracted heart and disordered brain dwells the source of that unhappiness which all the potentates on earth cannot relieve.

Let that man die unconsoled who can deride the invalid for undertaking a journey to distant, healthful springs, where he often finds only a heavier disease and a more painful death, or who can exult over the despairing mind of a sinner, who, to obtain peace of conscience and an alleviation of misery, makes a pilgrimage to the Holy Sepulchre. Each laborious step which galls his wounded feet in rough and untrodden paths pours a drop of balm into his troubled soul, and the journey of many a weary day brings a nightly relief to his anguished heart. Will you dare call this enthusiasm, ye crowd of pompous declaimers? Enthusiasm! O God! thou seest my tears. Thou hast allotted us our portion of misery: must we also have brethren to persecute us, to deprive us of our consolation, of our trust in thee, and in thy love and mercy? For our trust in the virtue of the healing root, or in the strength of the vine, what is it else than a belief in thee from whom all that surrounds us derives its healing and restoring powers? Father, whom I know not, —who wert once want to fill my soul but who now hidest thy face from me, —call me back to thee; be silent no longer; thy silence shall not delay a soul which thirsts after thee. What man, what father, could be angry with a son for returning to him suddenly, for falling on his neck, and exclaiming, "I am here again, my father! forgive me if I have anticipated my journey, and returned before the appointed time! The world is everywhere the same, —a scene of labour and pain, of pleasure and reward; but what does it all avail? I am happy only where thou art, and in thy presence am I content to suffer or enjoy." And wouldst thou, heavenly Father, banish such a child from thy presence?

DECEMBER 1.

Wilhelm, the man about whom I wrote to you—that man so enviable in his misfortunes—was secretary to Charlotte's father; and an unhappy passion for her which he cherished, concealed and at length discovered, caused him to be dismissed from his situation. This made him mad. Think, whilst you peruse this plain narration, what an impression the circumstance has made upon me! But it was related to me by Albert with as much calmness as you will probably peruse it.

DECEMBER 4.

I implore your attention. It is all over with me. I can support this state no longer. To-day I was sitting by Charlotte. She was playing upon her piano a succession of delightful melodies, with such intense expression! Her little sister was dressing her doll upon my lap. The tears came into my eyes. I leaned down and looked intently at her wedding ring: my tears fell—immediately she began to play that favourite, that divine, air which has so often enchanted me. I felt comfort from a recollection of the past, of those bygone days when that air was familiar to me; and then I recalled all the sorrows and the disappointments which I had since endured. I paced with hasty strides through the room, my heart became convulsed with painful emotions. At length I went up to her, and exclaimed with eagerness, "For Heaven's sake, play that air no longer!" She stopped and looked steadfastly at me. She then said, with a smile which sunk deep into my heart, "Werther, you are ill: your dearest food is distasteful to you. But go, I entreat you, and endeavour to compose yourself." I tore myself away. God, thou seest my torments, and wilt end them!

DECEMBER 6.

How her image haunts me! Waking or asleep, she fills my entire soul! Soon as I close my eyes, here, in my brain, where all the nerves of vision are concentrated, her dark eyes are imprinted. Here—I do not know how to describe it; but, if I shut my eyes, hers are immediately before me: dark as an abyss they open upon me and absorb my senses.

And what is man—that boasted demigod? Do not his powers fail when he most requires their use? And whether he soar in joy, or sink in sorrow, is not his career in both inevitably arrested? And, whilst he fondly dreams that he is grasping at infinity, does he not feel compelled to return to consciousness of his cold, monotonous existence?

THE EDITOR TO THE READER.

It is a matter of extreme regret that we want original evidence of the last remarkable days of our friend; and we are, therefore, obliged to interrupt the progress of his correspondence, and to supply the deficiency by a connected narration.

I have felt it my duty to collect accurate information from the mouths of persons well acquainted with his history. The story is simple; and all the accounts agree, except in some unimportant particulars. It is true that with respect to the characters of the persons spoken of opinions and judgments vary.

We have only, then, to relate conscientiously the facts which our diligent labour has enabled us to collect, to give the letters of the deceased, and to pay particular attention to the slightest fragment from his pen, more especially as it is so difficult to discover the real and correct motives of men who are not of the common order.

Sorrow and discontent had taken deep root in Werther's soul, and gradually imparted their character to his whole being. The harmony of his mind became completely disturbed; a perpetual excitement and mental irritation, which weakened his natural powers, produced the saddest effects upon him, and rendered him at length the victim of an exhaustion against which he struggled with still more painful efforts than he had displayed, even in contending with his other misfortunes. His mental anxiety weakened his various good qualities; and he was soon converted into a gloomy companion, always unhappy and unjust in his ideas, the more wretched he became. This was, at least, the opinion of Albert's friends. They assert, moreover, that the character of Albert himself had undergone no change in the meantime: he was still the same being whom Werther had loved, honoured and respected from commencement. His love for Charlotte was unbounded: he was proud of her, and desired that she should be recognized by everyone as the noblest of created beings. Was he, however, to blame for wishing to avert from her every appearance of suspicion? or for his unwillingness to share his rich prize with another, even for a moment, and in the most innocent manner? It is asserted that Albert frequently retired from his wife's apartment during Werther's visits; but this did not arise from hatred or aversion to his friend, but only from a feeling that his presence was oppressive to Werther.

Charlotte's father, who was confined to the house by indisposition, was accustomed to send his carriage for her, that she might make excursions in the neighbourhood. One day the weather had been unusually severe, and the whole country was covered with snow.

Werther went for Charlotte the following morning, in order that, if Albert were absent, he might conduct her home.

The beautiful weather produced but little impression on his

troubled spirit. A heavy weight lay upon his soul, deep melancholy had taken possession of him, and his mind knew no change save from one painful thought to another.

As he now never enjoyed internal peace, the condition of his fellow creatures was to him a perpetual source of trouble and distress. He believed he had disturbed the happiness of Albert and his wife; and, whilst he censured himself strongly for this, he began to entertain a secret dislike to Albert.

His thoughts were occasionally directed to this point. "Yes," he would repeat to himself, with ill-concealed dissatisfaction, "yes, this is, after all, the extent of that confiding, dear, tender, and sympathetic love, that calm and eternal fidelity! What do I behold but satiety and indifference? Does not every frivolous engagement attract him more than his charming and lovely wife? Does he know how to prize his happiness? Can he value her as she deserves? He possesses her, it is true, I know that, as I know much more, and I have become accustomed to the thought that he will drive me mad, or, perhaps, murder me. Is his friendship toward me unimpaired? Does he not view my attachment to Charlotte as an infringement upon his rights, and consider my attention to her as a silent rebuke to himself? I know, and indeed feel, that he dislikes me, that he wishes for my absence, that my presence is hateful to him."

He would often pause when on his way to visit Charlotte, stand still, as though in doubt, and seem desirous of returning, but would nevertheless proceed; and, engaged in such thoughts and soliloquies as we have described, he finally reached the hunting-lodge, with a sort of involuntary consent.

Upon one occasion he entered the house; and, inquiring for Charlotte, he observed that the inmates were in a state of unusual confusion. The eldest boy informed him that a dreadful misfortune had occurred at Walheim, —that a peasant had been murdered! But this made little impression upon him. Entering the apartment, he found Charlotte engaged reasoning with her father, who, in spite of his infirmity, insisted on going to the scene of the crime, in order to institute an inquiry. The criminal was unknown; the victim had been found dead at his own door that morning. Suspicions were excited: the murdered man had been in the service of a widow, and the person who had previously filled the situation had been dismissed from her employment.

As soon as Werther heard this, he exclaimed with great excitement, "Is it possible! I must go to the spot—I cannot delay a moment!" He hastened to Walheim. Every incident returned vividly to his remembrance; and he entertained not the slightest doubt that that man was the murderer to whom he had so often spoken, and for whom he entertained so much regard. His way took him past the well-known lime trees, to the house where the body had been carried; and his feelings were greatly excited at the sight of the fondly recollected spot. That threshold where the neighbours' children had so often played together was stained with blood; love and attachment, the noblest feelings of human nature, had been converted into violence and murder. The huge trees stood there leafless and covered with hoarfrost; the beautiful hedgerows which surrounded the old churchyard wall were withered; and the gravestones, half covered with snow, were visible through the openings.

As he approached the inn, in front of which the whole village was assembled, screams were suddenly heard. A troop of armed peasants was seen approaching and everyone exclaimed that the criminal had been apprehended. Werther looked and was not long in doubt. The prisoner was no other than the servant, who had been formerly so attached to the widow, and whom he had met prowling about, with that suppressed anger and ill-concealed despair, which we have before described.

"What have you done, unfortunate man?" inquired Werther, as he advanced toward the prisoner. The latter turned his eyes upon him in silence, and then replied with perfect composure; "No one will now marry her, and she will marry no one." The prisoner was taken into the inn, and Werther left the place. The mind of Werther was fearfully excited by this shocking occurrence. He ceased, however, to be oppressed by his usual feeling of melancholy, moroseness, and indifference to everything that passed around him. He entertained a strong degree of pity for the prisoner and was seized with an indescribable anxiety to save him from his impending fate. He considered him so unfortunate; he deemed his crime so excusable, and thought his own condition so nearly similar, that he felt convinced he could make everyone else view the matter in the light in which he saw it himself. He now became anxious to undertake his defence and commenced composing an eloquent speech for the occasion; and, on his way to the hunting-lodge, he could not refrain from speaking aloud the statement which he resolved to make to the judge.

Upon his arrival, he found Albert had been before him: and he was a little perplexed by this meeting; but he soon recovered himself and expressed his opinion with much warmth to the judge. The latter shook, his head doubtingly; and although Werther urged his case with the utmost zeal, feeling, and determination in defence of his client, yet, as we may easily suppose, the judge was not much influenced by his appeal. On the contrary, he interrupted him in his address, reasoned with him seriously, and even administered a rebuke to him for becoming the advocate of a murderer. He demonstrated, that, according to this precedent, every law might be violated, and the public security utterly destroyed. He added, moreover, that in such a case he could himself do nothing, without incurring the greatest responsibility; that everything must follow in the usual course and pursue the ordinary channel.

Werther, however, did not abandon his enterprise, and even besought the judge to connive at the flight of the prisoner. But this proposal was peremptorily rejected. Albert, who had taken some part in the discussion, coincided in opinion with the judge. At this Werther became enraged, and took his leave in great anger, after the judge had more than once assured him that the prisoner could not be saved.

The excess of his grief at this assurance may be inferred from a note we have found amongst his papers, and which was doubtless written upon this very occasion.

"You cannot be saved, unfortunate man! I see clearly that we cannot be saved!"

Werther was highly incensed at the observations which Albert had made to the judge in this matter of the prisoner. He thought he could detect therein a little bitterness toward himself personally; and although, upon reflection, it could not escape his sound judgment that their view of the matter was correct, he felt the greatest possible reluctance to make such an admission.

A memorandum of Werther's upon this point, expressive of his general feelings toward Albert, has been found amongst his papers.

"What is the use of my continually repeating that he is a good and estimable man? He is an inward torment to me, and I am incapable of being just toward him."

One fine evening in winter, when the weather seemed inclined to thaw, Charlotte and Albert were returning home together. The former looked from time to time about her, as if she missed Werther's company. Albert began to speak of him and censured him for his prejudices. He alluded to his unfortunate attachment, and wished it were possible to discontinue his acquaintance. "I desire it on our own account," he added; "and I request you will compel him to alter his deportment toward you, and to visit you less frequently. The world is censorious, and I know that here and there we are spoken of." Charlotte made no reply, and Albert seemed to feel her silence. At least, from that time he never again spoke of Werther; and, when she introduced the subject, he allowed the conversation to die away, or else he directed the discourse into another channel.

The vain attempt Werther had made to save the unhappy murderer was the last feeble glimmering of a flame about to be extinguished. He sank almost immediately afterward into a state of gloom and inactivity, until he was at length brought to perfect distraction by learning that he was to be summoned as a witness against the prisoner, who asserted his complete innocence.

His mind now became oppressed by the recollection of every misfortune of his past life. The mortification he had suffered at the ambassador's and his subsequent troubles, were revived in his memory. He became utterly inactive. Destitute of energy, he was cut off from every pursuit and occupation which compose the business of common life; and he became a victim to his own susceptibility, and to his restless passion for the most amiable and beloved of women, whose peace he destroyed. In this unvarying monotony of existence his days were consumed; and his powers became exhausted without aim or design, until they brought him to a sorrowful end.

A few letters which he left behind, and which we here subjoin, afford the best proofs of his anxiety of mind and of the depth of his passion, as well as of his doubts and struggles, and of his weariness of life.

DECEMBER 12.

Dear Wilhelm, I am reduced to the condition of those unfortunate wretches who believe they are pursued by an evil spirit. Sometimes I am oppressed, not by apprehension or fear, but by an inexpressible internal sensation, which weighs upon my heart, and impedes my breath! Then I wander forth at night, even in this tempestuous season, and feel pleasure in surveying the dreadful scenes around me.

Yesterday evening I went forth. A rapid thaw had suddenly set in, I had been informed that the river had risen, that the brooks had all overflowed their banks, and that the whole value of Walheim was under water! Upon the stroke of twelve I hastened forth. I beheld a fearful sight. The foaming torrents rolled from the mountains in the moonlight, —fields and meadows, trees, and hedges, were confounded together; and the entire valley was converted into a deep lake, which was agitated by the roaring wind! And when the moon shone forth, and tinged the black clouds with silver, and the impetuous torrent at my feet foamed and resounded with awful and grand impetuosity, I was overcome by a mingled sensation of apprehension and delight. With extended arms I looked down into the yawning abyss, and cried, "Plunge!'" For a moment my senses forsook me, in the intense delight of ending my sorrows and my sufferings by a plunge into that gulf! And then I felt as if I were rooted to the earth, and incapable of seeking an end to my woes! But my hour is not yet come, I feel it is not. O Wilhelm, how willingly could I abandon my existence to ride the whirlwind, or to embrace the torrent! and then might not rapture perchance be the portion of this liberated soul?

I turned my sorrowful eyes toward a favourite spot, where I was accustomed to sit with Charlotte beneath a willow after a fatiguing walk. Alas! it was covered with water, and with difficulty I found even the meadow. And the fields around the hunting-lodge, thought I. Has our dear bower been destroyed by this unpitying storm? And a beam of past happiness streamed upon me, as the mind of a captive is illumined by dreams of flocks and herds and bygone joys of home! But I am free from blame. I have courage to die! Perhaps I have, —but I still sit here, like a wretched pauper, who collects fagots, and begs her bread from door to door, that she may prolong for a few days a miserable existence which she is unwilling to resign.

DECEMBER 15.

What is the matter with me, dear Wilhelm? I am afraid of myself! Is not my love for her of the purest, most holy, and most brotherly nature? Has my soul ever been sullied by a single sensual desire? but I will make no protestations. And now, ye nightly visions, how truly have those mortals understood you, who ascribe your various contradictory effects to some invincible power! This night I tremble at the avowal—I held her in my arms, locked in a close embrace: I pressed her to my bosom, and covered with countless kisses those dear lips which murmured in reply to soft protestations of love. My sight became confused by the delicious intoxication of her eyes. Heavens! is it sinful to revel again in such happiness, to recall once more those rapturous moments with intense delight? Charlotte! Charlotte! I am lost! My senses are bewildered, my recollection is confused, mine eyes are bathed in tears—I am ill; and yet I am well—I wish for nothing—I have no desires—it were better I were gone.

Under the circumstances narrated above, a determination to quit this world had now taken fixed possession of Werther's soul. Since Charlotte's return, this thought had been the final object of all his hopes and wishes; but he had resolved that such a step should not be taken with precipitation, but with calmness and tranquility and with the most perfect deliberation.

His troubles and internal struggles may be understood from the following fragment, which was found, without any date, amongst his papers, and appears to have formed the beginning of a letter to Wilhelm.

"Her presence, her fate, her sympathy for me, have power still to extract tears from my withered brain.

"One lifts up the curtain, and passes to the other side, —that is all!

And why all these doubts and delays? Because we know not what is behind—because there is no returning—and because our mind infers that all is darkness and confusion, where we have nothing but uncertainty."

His appearance at length became quite altered by the effect of his melancholy thoughts; and his resolution was now finally and irrevocably taken, of which the following ambiguous letter, which he addressed to his friend, may appear to afford some proof.

DECEMBER 20.

I am grateful to your love, Wilhelm, for having repeated your advice so seasonably. Yes, you are right: it is undoubtedly better that I should depart. But I do not entirely approve your scheme of returning at once to your neighbourhood; at least, I should like to make a little excursion on the way, particularly as we may now expect a continued frost, and consequently good roads. I am much pleased with your intention of coming to fetch me; only delay your journey for a fortnight and wait for another letter from me. One should gather nothing before it is ripe, and a fortnight sooner or later makes a great difference. Entreat my mother to pray for her son and tell her I beg her pardon for all the unhappiness I have occasioned her. It has ever been my fate to give pain to those whose happiness I should have promoted. Adieu, my dearest friend. May every blessing of Heaven attend you! Farewell.

We find it difficult to express the emotions with which Charlotte's soul was agitated during the whole of this time, whether in relation to her husband or to her unfortunate friend; although we are enabled, by our knowledge of her character, to understand their nature.

It is certain that she had formed a determination, by every means in her power to keep Werther at a distance; and, if she hesitated in her decision, it was from a sincere feeling of friendly pity, knowing how much it would cost him, indeed, that he would find it almost impossible to comply with her wishes. But various causes now urged her to be firm. Her husband preserved a strict silence about the whole matter; and she never made it a subject of conversation, feeling bound to prove to him by her conduct that her sentiments agreed with his.

The same day, which was the Sunday before Christmas, after Werther had written the last-mentioned letter to his friend, he came in the evening to Charlotte's house, and found her alone. She was busy preparing some little gifts for her brothers and sisters, which were to be distributed to them on Christmas Day. He began talking of the delight of the children, and of that age when the sudden appearance of the Christmas-tree, decorated with fruit and sweetmeats, and lighted up with wax candles, causes such transports of joy. "You shall have a gift too, if you behave well," said Charlotte, hiding her embarrassment under sweet smile. "And what do you call behaving well? What should I do, what can I do, my dear Charlotte?" said he. "Thursday night," she answered, "is Christmas Eve. The children are all to be here, and my father too: there is a present for each; do you come likewise, but do not come before that time." Werther started. "I desire you will not: it must be so," she continued. "I ask it of you as a favour, for my own peace and tranquility. We cannot go on in this manner any longer." He turned away his face walked hastily up and down the room, muttering indistinctly, "We cannot go on in this manner any longer!" Charlotte, seeing the violent agitation into which these words had thrown him, endeavoured to divert his thoughts by different questions, but in vain. "No, Charlotte!" he exclaimed; "I will never see you anymore!" "And why so?" she answered. "We may—we must see each other again; only let it be with more discretion. Oh! why were you born with that excessive, that ungovernable passion for everything that is dear to you?" Then, taking his hand, she said, "I entreat of you to be calmer: your talents, your understanding, your genius, will furnish you with a thousand resources. Be a man and conquer an unhappy attachment toward a creature who can do nothing but pity you." He bit his lips and looked at her with a gloomy countenance. She continued to hold his hand. "Grant me but a moment's patience, Werther," she said. "Do you not see that you are deceiving yourself, that you are seeking your own destruction? Why must you love me, me only, who belong to another? I fear, I much fear, that it is only the impossibility of possessing me which makes your desire for me so strong." He drew back his hand, whilst he surveyed her with a wild and angry look. "'Tis well!" he exclaimed, "'tis very well! Did not Albert furnish you with this reflection? It is profound, a very profound remark." "A reflection that anyone might easily make," she answered, "and is there not a woman in the whole world who is at liberty, and has the power to make you happy? Conquer yourself: look for such a being and believe me when I say that you will certainly find her. I have long felt for you, and for us all: you have confined yourself too long within the limits of to narrow a circle. Conquer yourself; make an effort: a short journey will be of service to you. Seek and find an object worthy of your love; then return hither and let us enjoy together all the happiness of the most perfect friendship."

"This speech," replied Werther with a cold smile, "this speech should be printed, for the benefit of all teachers. My dear Charlotte, allow me but a short time longer, and all will be well." "But however, Werther," she added, "do not come again before Christmas." He was about to make some answer when Albert came in. They saluted each other coldly, and with mutual embarrassment paced up and down the room. Werther made some common remarks; Albert did the same, and their conversation soon dropped. Albert asked his wife about some household matters; and, finding that his commissions were not executed, he used some expressions which, to Werther's ear, savoured of extreme harshness. He wished to go but had no power to move and, in this situation, he remained till eight o'clock, his uneasiness and discontent continually increasing. At length the cloth was laid for supper, and he took up his hat and stick. Albert invited him to remain; but Werther, fancying that he was merely paying a formal compliment, thanked him coldly, and left the house.

Werther returned home, took the candle from his servant, and retired to his room alone. He talked for some time with great earnestness to himself, wept aloud, walked in a state of great excitement through his chamber; till at length, without undressing, he threw himself on the bed, where he was found by his servant at eleven o'clock, when the latter ventured to enter the room, and take off his boots. Werther did not prevent him but forbade him to come in the morning till he should ring.

On Monday morning, the 21st of December, he wrote to Charlotte the following letter, which was found, sealed, on his bureau after his death, and was given to her. I shall insert it in fragments; as it appears, from several circumstances, to have been written in that manner.

"It is all over, Charlotte: I am resolved to die! I make this declaration deliberately and coolly, without any romantic passion, on this morning of the day when I am to see you for the last time. At the moment you read these lines, O best of women, the cold grave will hold the inanimate remains of that restless and unhappy being who, in the last moments of his existence, knew no pleasure so great as that of conversing with you! I have passed a dreadful night or rather, let me say, a propitious one; for it has given me resolution, it has fixed my purpose. I am resolved to die. When I tore myself from you yesterday, my senses were in tumult and disorder; my heart was oppressed, hope and pleasure had fled from me forever, and a petrifying cold had seized my wretched being. I could scarcely reach my room. I threw myself on my knees; and Heaven, for the last time, granted me the consolation of shedding tears. A thousand ideas, a thousand schemes, arose within my soul; till at length one last, fixed, final thought took possession of my heart. It was to die. I lay down to rest; and in the morning, in the quiet hour of awakening, the same determination was upon me. To die! It is not despair: it is conviction that I have filled up the measure of my sufferings, that I have reached my appointed term, and must sacrifice myself for thee. Yes, Charlotte, why should I not avow it? One of us three must die: it shall be Werther. O beloved Charlotte! this heart, excited by rage and fury, has often conceived the horrid idea of murdering your husband—you—myself! The lot is cast at length. And in the bright, quiet evenings of summer, when you sometimes wander toward the mountains, let your thoughts then turn to me: recollect how often you have watched me coming to meet you from the valley; then bend your eyes upon the churchyard which contains my grave, and, by the light of the setting sun, mark how the evening breeze waves the tall grass which grows above my tomb. I was calm when I began this letter, but the recollection of these scenes makes me weep like a child."

About ten in the morning, Werther called his servant, and, whilst he was dressing, told him that in a few days he intended to set out upon a journey, and bade him therefore lay his clothes in order, and prepare them for packing up, call in all his accounts, fetch home the books he had lent, and give two months' pay to the poor dependents who were accustomed to receive from him a weekly allowance.

He breakfasted in his room, and then mounted his horse, and went to visit the steward, who, however, was not at home. He walked pensively in the garden, and seemed anxious to renew all the ideas that were most painful to him.

The children did not suffer him to remain alone long. They followed him, skipping and dancing before him, and told him, that after tomorrow and tomorrow and one day more, they were to receive their Christmas gift from Charlotte; and they then recounted all the wonders of which they had formed ideas in their child imaginations. "Tomorrow and tomorrow," said he, "and one day more!" And he kissed them tenderly. He was going; but the younger boy stopped him, to whisper something in his ear. He told him that his elder brothers had written splendid New-Year's wishes so large! one for papa, and another for Albert and Charlotte, and one for Werther; and they were to be presented early in the morning, on New Year's Day. This quite overcame him. He made each of the children a present, mounted his horse, left his compliments for papa and mamma, and, with tears in his eyes, rode away from the place.

He returned home about five o'clock, ordered his servant to keep up his fire, desired him to pack his books and linen at the bottom of the trunk, and to place his coats at the top. He then appears to have made the following addition to the letter addressed to Charlotte:

"You do not expect me. You think I will obey you, and not visit you again till Christmas Eve. O Charlotte, today or never! On Christmas Eve you will hold this paper in your hand; you will tremble and moisten it with your tears. I will—I must! Oh, how happy I feel to be determined!"

In the meantime, Charlotte was in a pitiable state of mind. After her last conversation with Werther, she found how painful to herself it would be to decline his visits and knew how severely he would suffer from their separation.

She had, in conversation with Albert, mentioned casually that Werther would not return before Christmas Eve; and soon afterward Albert went on horseback to see a person in the neighbourhood, with whom he had to transact some business which would detain him all night.

Charlotte was sitting alone. None of her family were near, and she gave herself up to the reflections that silently took possession of her mind. She was forever united to a husband whose love and fidelity she had proved, to whom she was heartily devoted, and who seemed to be a special gift from Heaven to ensure her happiness. On the other hand, Werther had become dear to her. There was a cordial unanimity of sentiment between them from the very first hour of their acquaintance, and their long association and repeated interviews had made an indelible impression upon her heart. She had been accustomed to communicate to him every thought and feeling which interested her, and his absence threatened to open a void in her existence which it might be impossible to fill. How heartily she wished that she might change him into her brother, —that she could induce him to marry one of her own friends or could reestablish his intimacy with Albert.

She passed all her intimate friends in review before her mind, but found something objectionable in each, and could decide upon none to whom she would consent to give him.

Amid all these considerations she felt deeply but indistinctly that her own real but unexpressed wish was to retain him for herself, and her pure and amiable heart felt from this thought a sense of oppression which seemed to forbid a prospect of happiness. She was wretched: a dark cloud obscured her mental vision.

It was now half-past six o'clock, and she heard Werther's step on the stairs. She at once recognized his voice, as he inquired if she were at home. Her heartbeat audibly—we could almost say for the first time—at his arrival. It was too late to deny herself; and, as he entered, she exclaimed, with a sort of ill-concealed confusion, "You have not kept your word!" "I promised nothing," he answered. "But you should have complied, at least for my sake," she continued. "I implore you, for both our sakes."

She scarcely knew what she said or did; and sent for some friends, who, by their presence, might prevent her being left alone with Werther. He put down some books he had brought with him, then made inquiries about some others, until she began to hope that her friends might arrive shortly, entertaining at the same time a desire that they might stay away.

At one moment she felt anxious that the servant should remain in the adjoining room, then she changed her mind. Werther, meanwhile, walked impatiently up and down. She went to the piano and determined not to retire. She then collected her thoughts, and sat down quietly at Werther's side, who had taken his usual place on the sofa.

"Have you brought nothing to read?" she inquired. He had nothing. "There in my drawer," she continued, "you will find your own translation of some of the songs of Ossian. I have not yet read them, as I have still hoped to hear you recite them; but, for some time past, I have not been able to accomplish such a wish." He smiled, and went for the manuscript, which he took with a shudder. He sat down; and, with eyes full of tears, he began to read.

"Star of descending night! fair is thy light in the west! thou liftest thy unshorn head from thy cloud; thy steps are stately on thy hill. What dost thou behold in the plain? The stormy winds are laid. The murmur of the torrent comes from afar. Roaring waves climb the distant rock. The flies of evening are on their feeble wings: the hum of their course is on the field. What dost thou behold, fair light? But thou dost smile and depart. The waves come with joy around thee: they bathe thy lovely hair. Farewell, thou silent beam! Let the light of Ossian's soul arise!

"And it does arise in its strength! I behold my departed friends. Their gathering is on Lora, as in the days of other years. Fingal comes like a watery column of mist! his heroes are around; and see the bards of song, gray-haired Ullin! stately Ryno! Alpin with the tuneful voice: the soft complaint of Minona! How are ye changed, my friends, since the days of Selma's feast! when we contended, like gales of spring as they fly along the hill, and bend by turns the feebly whistling grass.

"Minona came forth in her beauty, with downcast look and tearful eye. Her hair was flying slowly with the blast that rushed unfrequent from the hill. The souls of the heroes were sad when she raised the tuneful voice. Oft had they seen the grave of Salgar, the dark dwelling of white-bosomed Colma. Colma left alone on the hill with all her voice of song! Salgar promised to come! but the night descended around. Hear the voice of Colma when she sat alone on the hill!

"Colma. It is night: I am alone, forlorn on the hill of storms. The wind is heard on the mountain. The torrent is howling down the rock. No hut receives me from the rain: forlorn on the hill of winds!

"Rise moon! from behind thy clouds. Stars of the night, arise! Lead me, some light, to the place where my love rests from the chase alone! His bow near him unstrung, his dogs panting around him! But here I must sit alone by the rock of the mossy stream. The stream and the wind roar aloud. I hear not the voice of my love! Why delays my Salgar, why the chief of the hill his promise? Here is the rock and here the tree! here is the roaring stream! Thou didst promise with night to be here. Ah! whither is my Salgar gone? With thee I would fly from my father, with thee from my brother of pride. Our race have long been foes: we are not foes, O Salgar!

"Cease a little while, O wind! stream, be thou silent awhile! let my voice be heard around! let my wanderer hear me! Salgar! it is Colma who calls. Here is the tree and the rock. Salgar, my love, I am here! Why delayest thou thy coming? Lo! the calm moon comes forth. The flood is bright in the vale. The rocks are gray on the steep. I see him not on the brow. His dogs come not before him with tidings of his near approach. Here I must sit alone!

"Who lie on the heath beside me? Are they my love and my brother? Speak to me, O my friends! To Colma they give no reply. Speak to me: I am alone! My soul is tormented with fears. Ah, they are dead! Their swords are red from the fight. O my brother! my brother! why hast thou slain my Salgar! Why, O Salgar, hast thou slain my brother! Dear were ye both to me! what shall I say in your praise? Thou wert fair on the hill among thousands! he was terrible in fight! Speak to me! hear my voice! hear me, sons of my love! They are silent! silent forever! Cold, cold, are their breasts of clay! Oh, from the rock on the hill, from the top of the windy steep, speak, ye ghosts of the dead! Speak, I will not be afraid! Whither are ye gone to rest? In what cave of the hill shall I find the departed? No feeble voice is on the gale: no answer half drowned in the storm!

"I sit in my grief: I wait for morning in my tears! Rear the tomb, ye friends of the dead. Close it not till Colma come. My life flies away like a dream. Why should I stay behind? Here shall I rest with my friends, by the stream of the sounding rock. When night comes on the hill when the loud winds arise my ghost shall stand in the blast and mourn the death of my friends. The hunter shall hear from his booth; he shall fear but love my voice! For sweet shall my voice be for my friends: pleasant were her friends to Colma.

"Such was thy song, Minona, softly blushing daughter of Torman. Our tears descended for Colma, and our souls were sad! Ullin came with his harp; he gave the song of Alpin. The voice of Alpin was pleasant, the soul of Ryno was a beam of fire! But they had rested in the narrow house: their voice had ceased in Selma! Ullin had returned one day from the chase before the heroes fell. He heard their strife on the hill: their song was soft, but sad! They mourned the fall of Morar, first of mortal men! His soul was like the soul of Fingal: his sword like the sword of Oscar. But he fell, and his father mourned: his sister's eyes were full of tears. Minona's eyes were full of tears, the sister of car-borne Morar. She retired from the song of Ullin, like the moon in the west, when she foresees the shower, and hides her fair head in a cloud. I touched the harp with Ullin: the song of morning rose!

"Ryno. The wind and the rain are past, calm is the noon of day. The clouds are divided in heaven. Over the green hills flies the inconstant sun. Red through the stony vale comes down the stream of the hill. Sweet are thy murmurs, O stream! but sweeter is the voice I hear. It is the voice of Alpin, the son of song, mourning for the dead! Bent is his head of age: red his tearful eye. Alpin, thou son of song, why alone on the silent hill? why complainest thou, as a blast in the wood as a wave on the lonely shore?

"Alpin. My tears, O Ryno! are for the dead my voice for those that have passed away. Tall thou art on the hill; fair among the sons of the vale. But thou shalt fall like Morar:

the mourner shall sit on thy tomb. The hills shall know thee no more: thy bow shall lie in thy hall unstrung!

"Thou wert swift, O Morar! as a roe on the desert: terrible as a meteor of fire. Thy wrath was as the storm. Thy sword in battle as lightning in the field. Thy voice was as a stream after rain, like thunder on distant hills. Many fell by thy arm: they were consumed in the flames of thy wrath. But when thou didst return from war, how peaceful was thy brow. Thy face was like the sun after rain: like the moon in the silence of night: calm as the breast of the lake when the loud wind is laid.

"Narrow is thy dwelling now! dark the place of thine abode! With three steps I compass thy grave, O thou who wast so great before! Four stones, with their heads of moss, are the only memorial of thee. A tree with scarce a leaf, long grass which whistles in the wind, mark to the hunter's eye the grave of the mighty Morar. Morar! thou art low indeed. Thou hast no mother to mourn thee, no maid with her tears of love. Dead is she that brought thee forth. Fallen is the daughter of Morglan.

"Who on his staff is this? Who is this whose head is white with age, whose eyes are red with tears, who quakes at every step? It is thy father, O Morar! the father of no son but thee. He heard of thy fame in war, he heard of foes dispersed. He heard of Morar's renown, why did he not hear of his wound? Weep, thou father of Morar! Weep, but thy son heareth thee not. Deep is the sleep of the dead, low their pillow of dust. No more shall he hear thy voice, no more awake at thy call. When shall it be morn in the grave, to bid the slumberer awake? Farewell, thou bravest of men! thou conqueror in the field! but the field shall see thee no more, nor the dark wood be lightened with the splendour of thy steel. Thou has left no son. The song shall preserve thy name. Future times shall hear of thee they shall hear of the fallen Morar!

"The grief of all arose, but most the bursting sigh of Armin. He remembers the death of his son, who fell in the days of his youth. Carmor was near the hero, the chief of the echoing Galmal. Why burst the sigh of Armin? he said. Is there a cause to mourn? The song comes with its music to melt and please the soul. It is like soft mist that, rising from a lake, pours on the silent vale; the green flowers are filled with dew, but the sun returns in his strength, and the mist is gone. Why art thou sad, O Armin, chief of sea-surrounded Gorma?

"Sad I am! nor small is my cause of woe! Carmor, thou hast lost no son; thou hast lost no daughter of beauty. Colgar the valiant lives, and Annira, fairest maid. The boughs of thy house ascend, O Carmor! but Armin is the last of his race. Dark is thy bed, O Daura! deep thy sleep in the tomb! When shalt thou wake with thy songs? with all thy voice of music?

"Arise, winds of autumn, arise blow along the heath. Streams of the mountains, roar; roar, tempests in the groves of my oaks! Walk through broken clouds, O moon! show thy pale face at intervals; bring to my mind the night when all my children fell, when Arindal the mighty fell—when Daura the lovely failed. Daura, my daughter, thou wert fair, fair as the moon on Fura, white as the driven snow, sweet as the breathing gale. Arindal, thy bow was strong, thy spear was swift on the field, thy look was like mist on the wave, thy shield a red cloud in a storm! Armar, renowned in war, came and sought Daura's love. He was not long refused: fair was the hope of their friends.

"Erath, son of Odgal, repined: his brother had been slain by Armar. He came disguised like a son of the sea: fair was his cliff on the wave, white his locks of age, calm his serious brow. Fairest of women, he said, lovely daughter of Armin! a rock not distant in the sea bears a tree on its side; red shines the fruit afar. There Armar waits for Daura. I come to carry his love! she went she called on Armar. Nought answered, but the son of the rock. Armar, my love, my love! why tormentest thou me with fear? Hear, son of Arnart, hear! it is Daura who calleth thee. Erath, the traitor, fled laughing to the land. She lifted up her voice—she called for her brother and her father. Arindal! Armin! none to relieve you, Daura.

"Her voice came over the sea. Arindal, my son, descended from the hill, rough in the spoils of the chase. His arrows rattled by his side; his bow was in his hand, five dark-gray dogs attended his steps. He saw fierce Erath on the shore; he seized and bound him to an oak. Thick wind the thongs of the hide around his limbs; he loads the winds with his groans. Arindal ascends the deep in his boat to bring Daura to land. Armar came in his wrath and let fly the gray-feathered shaft. It sung, it sunk in thy heart, O Arindal, my son! for Erath the traitor thou diest. The oar is stopped at once: he panted on the rock and expired. What is thy grief, O Daura, when round thy feet is poured thy brother's blood. The boat is broken in twain. Armar plunges into the sea to rescue his Daura or die. Sudden a blast from a hill came over the waves; he sank, and he rose no more.

"Alone, on the sea-beat rock, my daughter was heard to complain; frequent and loud were her cries. What could her father do? All night I stood on the shore: I saw her by the faint beam of the moon. All night I heard her cries. Loud was the wind; the rain beat hard on the hill. Before morning appeared, her voice was weak; it died away like the evening breeze among the grass of the rocks. Spent with grief, she expired, and left thee, Armin, alone. Gone is my strength in war, fallen my pride among women. When the storms aloft arise, when the north lifts the wave on high, I sit by the sounding shore, and look on the fatal rock.

"Often by the setting moon I see the ghosts of my children; half viewless they walk in mournful conference together."

A torrent of tears which streamed from Charlotte's eyes and gave relief to her bursting heart, stopped Werther's recitation. He threw down the book, seized her hand, and wept bitterly. Charlotte leaned upon her hand and buried her face in her handkerchief: the agitation of both was excessive. They felt that their own fate was pictured in the misfortunes of Ossian's heroes, they felt this together, and their tears redoubled. Werther supported his forehead on Charlotte's arm: she trembled, she wished to be gone; but sorrow and sympathy lay like a leaden weight upon her soul. She recovered herself shortly, and begged Werther, with broken sobs, to leave her, implored him with the utmost earnestness to comply with her request. He trembled; his heart was ready to burst then, taking up the book again, he recommended reading, in a voice broken by sobs.

"Why dost thou waken me, O spring? Thy voice woos me, exclaiming, I refresh thee with heavenly dews; but the time of my decay is approaching, the storm is nigh that shall whither my leaves. Tomorrow the traveller shall come, he shall come, who beheld me in beauty: his eye shall seek me in the field around, but he shall not find me."

The whole force of these words fell upon the unfortunate Werther. Full of despair, he threw himself at Charlotte's feet, seized her hands, and pressed them to his eyes and to his forehead. An apprehension of his fatal project now struck her for the first time. Her senses were bewildered: she held his hands, pressed them to her bosom; and, leaning toward him with emotions of the tenderest pity, her warm cheek touched his. They lost sight of everything. The world disappeared from their eyes. He clasped her in his arms, strained her to his bosom, and covered her trembling lips with passionate kisses. "Werther!" she cried with a faint voice, turning herself away; "Werther!" and, with a feeble hand, she pushed him from her. At length, with the firm voice of virtue, she exclaimed, "Werther!" He resisted not, but, tearing himself from her arms, fell on his knees before her. Charlotte rose, and, with disordered grief, in mingled tones of love and resentment, she exclaimed, "It is the last time, Werther! You shall never see me anymore!" Then, casting one last, tender look upon her unfortunate lover, she rushed into the adjoining room, and locked the door. Werther held out his arms but did not dare to detain her. He continued on the ground, with his head resting on the sofa, for half an hour, till he heard a noise which brought him to his senses. The servant entered. He then walked up and down the room; and, when he was again left alone, he went to Charlotte's door, and, in a low voice, said, "Charlotte, Charlotte! but one word more, one last adieu!" She returned no answer. He stopped and listened and entreated; but all was silent. At length he tore himself from the place, crying, "Adieu, Charlotte, adieu forever!"

Werther ran to the gate of the town. The guards, who knew him, let him pass in silence. The night was dark and stormy, —it rained and snowed. He reached his own door about eleven. His servant, although seeing him enter the house without his hat, did not venture to say anything and as he undressed his master, he found that his clothes were wet. His hat was afterward found on the point of a rock overhanging the valley; and it is inconceivable how he could have climbed to the summit on such a dark, tempestuous night without losing his life.

He retired to bed and slept to a late hour. The next morning his servant, upon being called to bring his coffee, found him writing.

He was adding, to Charlotte, what we here annex.

"For the last, last time I open these eyes. Alas! they will behold the sun no more. It is covered by a thick, impenetrable cloud. Yes, Nature! put on mourning: your child, your friend, your lover, draws near his end! This thought, Charlotte, is without parallel; and yet it seems like a mysterious dream when I repeat—this is my last day! The last! Charlotte, no word can adequately express this thought. The last! Today I stand erect in all my strength tomorrow, cold, and stark, I shall lie extended upon the ground. To die! what is death? We do but dream in our discourse upon it. I have seen many human beings die but so straitened is our feeble nature, we have no clear conception of the beginning or the end of our existence. At this moment I am my own—or rather I am thine, thine, my adored! and the next we are parted, severed—perhaps forever! No, Charlotte, no! How can I, how can you, be annihilated? We exist. What is annihilation? A mere word, an unmeaning sound that fixes no impression on the mind. Dead, Charlotte! laid in the cold earth, in the dark and narrow grave! I had a friend once who was everything to me in early youth. She died. I followed her hearse; I stood by her grave when the coffin was lowered; and when I heard the creaking of the cords as they were loosened and drawn up, when the first shovelful of earth was thrown in, and the coffin returned a hollow sound, which grew fainter and fainter till all was completely covered over, I threw myself on the ground; my heart was smitten, grieved, shattered, rent—but I neither knew what had happened, nor what was to happen to me. Death! the grave! I understand not the words. —Forgive, oh, forgive me! Yesterday—ah, that day should have been the last of my life! Thou angel! for the first time in my existence, I felt rapture glow within my inmost soul. She loves, she loves me! Still burns upon my lips the sacred fire they received from thine. New torrents of delight overwhelm my soul. Forgive me, oh, forgive!

"I knew that I was dear to you; I saw it in your first entrancing look, knew it by the first pressure of your hand; but when I was absent from you, when I saw Albert at your side, my doubts and fears returned.

"Do you remember the flowers you sent me, when, at that crowded assembly, you could neither speak nor extend your hand to me? Half the night I was on my knees before those flowers, and I regarded them as the pledges of your love; but those impressions grew fainter and were at length effaced.

"Everything passes away; but a whole eternity could not extinguish the living flame which was yesterday kindled by your lips, and which now burns within me. She loves me! These arms have encircled her waist, these lips have trembled upon hers. She is mine! Yes, Charlotte, you are mine forever!

"And what do they mean by saying Albert is your husband? He may be so for this world; and in this world it is a sin to love you, to wish to tear you from his embrace. Yes, it is a crime; and I suffer the punishment, but I have enjoyed the full delight of my sin. I have inhaled a balm that has revived my soul. From this hour you are mine; yes, Charlotte, you are mine! I go before you. I go to my Father and to your Father. I will pour out my sorrows before him, and he will give me comfort till you arrive. Then will I fly to meet you. I will claim you, and remain your eternal embrace, in the presence of the Almighty.

"I do not dream; I do not rave. Drawing nearer to the grave my perceptions become clearer. We shall exist; we shall see each other again; we shall behold your mother; I shall behold her and expose to her my inmost heart. Your mother—your image!"

About eleven o'clock Werther asked his servant if Albert had returned. He answered, "Yes;" for he had seen him pass on horseback: upon which Werther sent him the following note, unsealed:

"Be so good as to lend me your pistols for a journey. Adieu."

Charlotte had slept little during the past night. All her apprehensions were realized in a way that she could neither foresee nor avoid. Her blood was boiling in her veins, and a thousand painful sensations rent her pure heart. Was it the ardour of Werther's passionate embraces that she felt within her bosom? Was it anger at his daring? Was it the sad comparison of her present condition with former days of innocence, tranquility, and self-confidence? How could she approach her husband, and confess a scene which she had no reason to conceal, and which she yet felt, nevertheless, unwilling to avow? They had preserved so long a silence toward each-other and should she be the first to break it by so unexpected a discovery? She feared that the mere statement of Werther's visit would trouble him, and his distress would be heightened by her perfect candour. She wished that he could see her in her true light, and judge her without prejudice; but was she anxious that he should read her inmost soul? On the other hand, could she deceive a being to whom all her thoughts had ever been exposed as clearly as crystal, and from whom no sentiment had ever been concealed? These reflections made her anxious and thoughtful. Her mind still dwelt on Werther, who was now lost to her, but whom she could not bring herself to resign, and for whom she knew nothing was left but despair if she should be lost to him forever.

A recollection of that mysterious estrangement which had lately subsisted between herself and Albert, and which she could never thoroughly understand, was now beyond measure painful to her. Even the prudent and the good have before now hesitated to explain their mutual differences, and have dwelt in silence upon their imaginary grievances, until circumstances have become so entangled, that in that critical juncture, when a calm explanation would have saved all parties, an understanding was impossible. And thus, if domestic confidence had been earlier established between them, if love and kind forbearance had mutually animated and expanded their hearts, it might not, perhaps, even yet have been too late to save our friend.

But we must not forget one remarkable circumstance. We may observe from the character of Werther's correspondence, that he had never affected to conceal his anxious desire to quit this world. He had often discussed the subject with Albert; and, between the latter and Charlotte, it had not unfrequently formed a topic of conversation. Albert was so opposed to the very idea of such an action, that, with a degree of irritation unusual in him, he had more than once given Werther to understand that he doubted the seriousness of his threats, and not only turned them into ridicule, but caused Charlotte to share his feelings of incredulity. Her heart was thus tranquilized when she felt disposed to view the melancholy subject in a serious point of view, though she never communicated to her husband the apprehensions she sometimes experienced.

Albert, upon his return, was received by Charlotte with ill-concealed embarrassment. He was himself out of humour; his business was unfinished; and he had just discovered that the neighbouring official with whom he had to deal, was an obstinate and narrow-minded personage. Many things had occurred to irritate him.

He inquired whether anything had happened during his absence, and Charlotte hastily answered that Werther had been there on the evening previously. He then inquired for his letters and was answered that several packages had been left in his study. He thereon retired, leaving Charlotte alone.

The presence of the being she loved and honoured produced a new impression on her heart. The recollection of his generosity, kindness, and affection had calmed her agitation: a secret impulse prompted her to follow him; she took her work and went to his study, as was often her custom. He was busily employed opening and reading his letters. It seemed as if the contents of some were disagreeable. She asked some questions: he gave short answers and sat down to write.

Several hours passed in this manner, and Charlotte's feelings became more and more melancholy. She felt the extreme difficulty of explaining to her husband, under any circumstances, the weight that lay upon her heart; and her depression became every moment greater, in proportion as she endeavoured to hide her grief, and to conceal her tears.

The arrival of Werther's servant occasioned her the greatest embarrassment. He gave Albert a note, which the latter coldly handed to his wife, saying, at the same time, "Give him the pistols. I wish him a pleasant journey," he added, turning to the servant. These words fell upon Charlotte like a thunderstroke: she rose from her seat half-fainting, and unconscious of what she did. She walked mechanically toward the wall, took down the pistols with a trembling hand, slowly wiped the dust from them, and would have delayed longer, had not Albert hastened her movements by an impatient look. She then delivered the fatal weapons to the servant, without being able to utter a word. As soon as he had departed, she folded up her work, and retired at once to her room, her heart overcome with the most fearful forebodings. She anticipated some dreadful calamity. She was at one moment on the point of going to her husband, throwing herself at his feet, and acquainting him with all that had happened on the previous evening, that she might acknowledge her fault, and explain her apprehensions; then she saw that such a step would be useless, as she would certainly be unable to induce Albert to visit Werther. Dinner was served; and a kind friend whom she had persuaded to remain assisted to sustain the conversation, which was carried on by a sort of compulsion, till the events of the morning were forgotten.

When the servant brought the pistols to Werther, the latter received them with transports of delight upon hearing that Charlotte had given them to him with her own hand. He ate some bread, drank some wine, sent his servant to dinner, and then sat down to write as follows:

"They have been in your hands you wiped the dust from them. I kiss them a thousand times—you have touched them. Yes, Heaven favours my design, and you, Charlotte, provide me with the fatal instruments. It was my desire to receive my death from your hands, and my wish is gratified. I have made inquiries of my servant. You trembled when you gave him the pistols, but you bade me no adieu. Wretched, wretched that I am—not one farewell! How could you shut your heart against me in that hour which makes you mine forever? Charlotte, ages cannot efface the impression—I feel you cannot hate the man who so passionately loves you!"

After dinner he called his servant, desired him to finish the packing up, destroyed many papers, and then went out to pay some trifling debts. He soon returned home, then went out again, notwithstanding the rain, walked for some time in the count's garden, and afterward proceeded farther into the country. Toward evening he came back once more and resumed his writing.

"Wilhelm, I have for the last time beheld the mountains, the forests, and the sky. Farewell! And you, my dearest mother, forgive me! Console her, Wilhelm. God bless you! I have settled all my affairs! Farewell! We shall meet again and be happier than ever."

"I have requited you badly, Albert; but you will forgive me. I have disturbed the peace of your home. I have sowed distrust between you. Farewell! I will end all this wretchedness. And oh, that my death may render you happy! Albert, Albert! make that angel happy, and the blessing of Heaven be upon you!"

He spent the rest of the evening in-arranging his papers: he tore and burned a great many others he sealed up and directed to

Wilhelm. They contained some detached thoughts and maxims, some of which I have perused. At ten o'clock he ordered his fire to be made up, and a bottle of wine to be brought to him. He then dismissed his servant, whose room, as well as the apartments of the rest of the family, was situated in another part of the house. The servant lay down without undressing, that he might be the sooner ready for his journey in the morning, his master having informed him that the post-horses would be at the door before six o'clock.

"Past eleven o'clock! All is silent around me, and my soul is calm. I thank thee, O God, that thou bestowest strength and courage upon me in these last moments! I approach the window, my dearest of friends; and through the clouds, which are at this moment driven rapidly along by the impetuous winds, I behold the stars which illumine the eternal heavens. No, you will not fall, celestial bodies: the hand of the Almighty supports both you and me! I have looked for the last time upon the constellation of the Greater Bear: it is my favourite star; for when I bade you farewell at night, Charlotte, and turned my steps from your door, it always shone upon me. With what rapture have I at times beheld it! How often have I implored it with uplifted hands to witness my felicity! and even still—But what object is there, Charlotte, which fails to summon up your image before me? Do you not surround me on all sides? and have I not, like a child, treasured up every trifle which you have consecrated by your touch?

"Your profile, which was so dear to me, I return to you; and I pray you to preserve it. Thousands of kisses have I imprinted upon it, and a thousand times has it gladdened my heart on departing from and returning to my home.

"I have implored your father to protect my remains. At the corner of the churchyard, looking toward the fields, there are two lime-trees—there I wish to lie. Your father can, and doubtless will, do this much for his friend. Implore it of him. But perhaps pious

Christians will not choose that their bodies should be buried near the corpse of a poor, unhappy wretch like me. Then let me be laid in some remote valley, or near the highway, where the priest and Levite may bless themselves as they pass by my tomb, whilst the Samaritan will shed a tear for my fate.

"See, Charlotte, I do not shudder to take the cold and fatal cup, from which I shall drink the draught of death. Your hand presents it to me, and I do not tremble. All, all is now concluded: the wishes and the hopes of my existence are fulfilled. With cold, unflinching hand I knock at the brazen portals of Death. Oh, that I had enjoyed the bliss of dying for you! how gladly would I have sacrificed myself for you; Charlotte! And could I but restore peace and joy to your bosom, with what resolution, with what joy, would I not meet my fate! But it is the lot of only a chosen few to shed their blood for their friends, and by their death to augment, a thousand times, the happiness of those by whom they are beloved.

"I wish, Charlotte, to be buried in the dress I wear at present: it has been rendered sacred by your touch. I have begged this favour of your father. My spirit soars above my sepulchre. I do not wish my pockets to be searched. The knot of pink ribbon which you wore on your bosom the first time I saw you, surrounded by the children—Oh, kiss them a thousand times for me, and tell them the fate of their unhappy friend! I think I see them playing around me. The dear children! How warmly have I been attached to you, Charlotte! Since the first hour I saw you, how impossible have I found it to leave you. This ribbon must be buried with me: it was a present from you on my birthday. How confused it all appears! Little did I then think that I should journey this road. But peace! I pray you, peace!

"They are loaded—the clock strikes twelve. I say amen. Charlotte, Charlotte! farewell, farewell!"

A neighbour saw the flash, and heard the report of the pistol; but, as everything remained quiet, he thought no more of it.

In the morning, at six o'clock, the servant went into Werther's room with a candle. He found his master stretched upon the floor, weltering in his blood, and the pistols at his side. He called, he took him in his arms, but received no answer. Life was not yet quite extinct. The servant ran for a surgeon and then went to fetch Albert. Charlotte heard the ringing of the bell: a cold shudder seized her. She wakened her husband, and they both rose. The servant, bathed in tears faltered forth the dreadful news. Charlotte fell senseless at Albert's feet.

When the surgeon came to the unfortunate Werther, he was still lying on the floor; and his pulse beat, but his limbs were cold. The bullet, entering the forehead, over the right eye, had penetrated the skull. A vein was opened in his right arm: the blood came, and he still continued to breathe.

From the blood which flowed from the chair, it could be inferred that he had committed the rash act sitting at his bureau, and that he afterward fell upon the floor. He was found lying on his back near the window. He was in a full-dress costume.

The house, the neighbourhood, and the whole town were immediately in commotion. Albert arrived. They had laid Werther on the bed: his head was bound up, and the paleness of death was upon his face. His limbs were motionless; but he still breathed, at one time strongly, then weaker—his death was momently expected.

He had drunk only one glass of the wine. "Emilia Galotti" lay open upon his bureau.

I shall say nothing of Albert's distress, or of Charlotte's grief.

The old steward hastened to the house immediately upon hearing the news: he embraced his dying friend amid a flood of tears. His eldest boys soon followed him on foot. In speechless sorrow they threw themselves on their knees by the bedside and kissed his hands and face. The eldest, who was his favourite, hung over him till he expired; and even then, he was removed by force. At twelve o'clock Werther breathed his last. The presence of the steward, and the precautions he had adopted, prevented a disturbance; and that night, at the hour of eleven, he caused the body to be interred in the place which Werther had selected for himself.

The steward and his sons followed the corpse to the grave. Albert was unable to accompany them. Charlotte's life was despaired of. The body was carried by labourers. No priest attended.

LIST OF TITLES WITH ISBN NO.

ISBN	TITLE
9788194914129	1984
9789390575220	1984 & Animal Farm (2In1)
9789390575572	1984 & Animal Farm (2In1): The International Best-Selling Classics
9789390575848	35 Sonnets
9789390575329	A Clergyman's Daughter
9789390575923	A Study In Scarlet
9789390896097	A Tale Of Two Cities
9789390896837	Abide in Christ
9789390896202	Abraham Lincoln
9789390896912	Absolute Surrender
9789390896608	African American Classic Collection
9789390575305	Aldous Huxley: The Collected Works
9789390896141	An Autobiography of M. K. Gandhi
9789390575886	Animal Farm
9789390575619	Animal Farm & The Great Gatsby (2In1)
9789390575626	Animal Farm & We
9789390896158	Anna Karenina
9789390575534	Antic Hay
9789390896165	Antony & Cleopatra
9789390896172	As I Lay Dying
9789390896226	As You like it
9789390575671	At Your Command
9789390575350	Awakened Imagination
9789390575114	Be What You Wish
9789390896233	Believe In yourself
9789390896998	Best of Charles Darwin: The Origin of Species & Autobiography
9789390896684	Best Of Horror : Dracula And Frankenstein
9789390575503	Best Of Mark Twain (The Adventures of Tom Sawyer AND The Adventures of Huckleberry Finn)
9789390896769	Black History Collection
9789390575756	Brave New World, Animal Farm & 1984 (3in1)

9789390896240	Brother Karamzov
9789390575053	Bulleh Shah Poetry
9789390575725	Burmese Days
9789390896257	Bushido
9789390896066	Can't Hurt Me
9788194914112	Chanakya Neeti: With The Complete Sutras
9789390896042	Crime and Punishment
9789390575527	Crome Yellow
9789390575046	Down and Out in Paris and London
9789390896844	Dracula
9789390575442	Emersons Essays: The Complete First & Second Series (Self-Reliance & Other Essays)
9789390575749	Emma
9789390575817	Essential Tozer Collection - The Pursuit of God & The Purpose of Man
9789390896578	Fascism What It Is and How to Fight It
9789390575688	Feeling is the Secret
9789390575190	Five Lessons
9789390575954	Frankenstein
9789390575237	Franz Kafka: Collected Works
9789390575282	Franz Kafka: Short Stories
9789390575060	George Orwell Collected Works
9789390575077	George Orwell Essays
9789390575213	George Orwell Poems
9788194914150	Greatest Poetry Ever Written Vol 1
9788194914143	Greatest Poetry Ever Written Vol 1
9789390896301	Gulliver's Travel
9789390575961	Gunaho Ka Devta
9789390575893	H. P. Lovecraft Selected Stories Vol 1
9789390575978	H. P. Lovecraft Selected Stories Vol 2
9789390896059	Hamlet
9789390575022	His Last Bow: Some Reminiscences of Sherlock Holmes
9789390896134	History of Western Philosophy
9789390575121	Homage To Catalonia

9789390896219	How to develop self-confidence and Improve public Speaking
9789390896295	How to enjoy your life and your Job
9789390575633	How to own your own mind
9789390896318	How to read Human Nature
9789390896325	How to sell your way through the life
9789390896370	How to use the laws of mind
9789390896387	How to use the power of prayer
9789390896028	How to win friends & Influence People
9788194824176	How To Win Friends and Influence People
9789390896103	Humility The Beauty of Holiness
9789390896653	Imperialism the Highest Stage of Capitalism
9789390575084	In Our Time
9789390575169	In Our Time & Three Stories and Ten poems
9789390575145	James Allen: The Collected Works
9789390896189	Jesus Himself
9789390575480	Jo's Boys
9789390896394	Julius Caesar
9789390575404	Keep the Aspidistra Flying
9789390896400	Kidnapped
9789390896424	King Lear
9789390575824	Lady Susan
9789390896455	Law of Success
9789390896264	Lincoln The Unknown
9789390575565	Little Men
9789390575640	Little Women
9788194914174	Lost Horizon
9789390896462	Macbeth
9789390896929	Man Eaters of Kumaon
9789390896523	Man The Dwelling Place of God
9789390896349	Man The Dwelling Place of God
9789390575909	Mansfield Park
9788194914136	Manto Ki 25 Sarvshreshth Kahaniya
9789390896509	Marxism, Anarchism, Communism
9789390575664	Mathematical Principles of Natural Philosophy

9788194914198	Meditations
9789390575800	Mein Kampf
9789390575794	Memory How To Develop, Train, And Use It
9789390896486	Mind Power
9789390896585	Money
9789390575039	Mortal Coils
9789390575770	My Life and Work
9789390896035	Narrative of the Life of Frederick Douglass
9789390575152	Neville Goddard: The Collected Works
9789390575985	Northanger Abbey
9789390896530	Notes From Underground
9789390896547	Oliver Twist
9789390575459	On War
9789390575541	One, None and a Hundred Thousand
9789390896554	Othelo
9789390575435	Out Of This World
9789390575015	Persuasion
9789390575510	Prayer The Art Of Believing
9789390575091	Pride and Prejudice
9789390896561	Psychic Perception
9789390575381	Rabindranath Tagore - 5 Best Short Stories Vol 2
9789390575367	Rabindranath Tagore - Short Stories (Masters Collections Including The Childs Return)
9789390575374	Rabindranath Tagore 5 Best Short Stories Vol 1 (Including The Childs Return
9789390896622	Romeo & Juliet
9789390896127	Sanatana Dharma
9789390575596	Seedtime & Harvest
9789390896639	Selected Stories of Guy De Maupassant
9789390575206	Self-Reliance & Other Essays
9789390575176	Sense and Sensibility
9789390575299	Shyamchi Aai
9789390896738	Socialism Utopian and Scientific
9789390896646	Success Through a Positive Mental Attitude
9789390575428	The Adventures of Huckleberry Finn

9789390575183	The Adventures of Sherlock Holmes
9789390575343	The Adventures of Tom Sawyer
9789390896691	The Alchemy Of Happiness
9789390575862	The Art Of Public Speaking
9789390896288	The Autobiography Of Charles Darwin
9788194914181	The Best of Franz Kafka: The Metamorphosis & The Trial
9789390575008	The Call Of Cthulhu and Other Weird Tales
9789390575107	The Case-Book of Sherlock Holmes
9789390896110	The Castle Of Otranto
9789390896745	The Communist Manifesto
9789390575589	The Complete Fiction of H. P. Lovecraft
9789390575497	The Complete Works of Florence Scovel Shinn
9789390896820	The Conquest of Breard
9789390896813	The Diary of a Young Girl
9789390896332	The Diary of a Young Girl The Definitive Edition of the Worlds Most Famous Diary
9789390575701	The Great Gatsby, Animal Farm & 1984 (3In1)
9789390575312	The Greatest Works Of George Orwell (5 Books) Including 1984 & Non-Fiction
9789390575992	The Hound of Baskervilles
9789390896707	The Idiot
9789390896714	The Invisible Man
9789390575657	The Knowledge of the holy
9789390575558	The Law & the Promise
9789390896721	The Law Of Attraction
9789390896776	The Leader in you
9789390896363	The Life of Christ
9789390896196	The Man-Eating Leopard of Rudraprayag
9789390896783	The Master Key to Riches
9789390575268	The Memoirs Of Sherlock Holmes
9789390896479	The Midsummer Night's Dream
9789390575466	The Mill On The Floss
9789390896790	The Miracles of your mind
9789390896660	The Mutual Aid A Factor in Evolution
9789390896448	The Origin of Species

9789390896905	The Peter Kropotkin Anthology The Conquest of Bread & Mutual Aid A Factor of Evolution
9789390896806	The Picture of Dorian Gray
9789390896271	The Picture of Dorian Gray
9789390575275	The Power Of Awareness
9789390896356	The Power of Concentration
9788194824169	The Power of Positive Thinking
9789390575411	The Power of the Spoken Word
9788194914105	The Power Of Your Subconscious Mind
9789390896899	The Power of Your Subconscious Mind
9789390896417	The Principles of Communism
9789390575787	The Psychology Of Mans Possible Evolution
9789390896615	The Psychology of Salesmanship
9789390575732	The Pursuit of God
9789390575398	The Pursuit of Happiness
9789390896851	The Quick and Easy Way to effective Speaking
9789390575947	The Return Of Sherlock Holmes
9789390575138	The Road To Wigan Pier
9789390896981	The Root of the Righteous
9789390575855	The Science Of Being Well
9788194914167	The Science Of Getting Rich, The Science Of Being Great & The Science Of Being Well (3In1)
9789390896011	The Screwtape Letters
9789390896073	The Screwtape Letters
9789390575336	The Secret Door to Success
9789390575695	The Secret Of Imagining
9789390896868	The Secret Of Success
9789390896431	The Seven Last Words
9789390575930	The Sign of the Four
9789390896004	The Sonnets
9789390896516	The Souls of Black Folk
9789390896875	The Sound and The Fury
9789390575244	The State and Revolution
9789390896882	The Story of My Life
9789390896936	The Story Of Oriental Philosophy

9789390896752	The Strange Case of Dr. Jekyll and Mr. Hyde
9789390896943	The Tempest
9789390575916	The Valley Of Fear
9789390575879	The Wind in the willows
9789390896080	The Wind in the willows
9789390575763	Their eyes were watching gofd
9789390575831	Three Stories
9789390896950	Twelfth Night
9789390896592	Twelve Years a Slave
9789390896677	Up from Slavery
9789390896974	Value Price and Profit
9789390896967	Wake Up and Live
9789390896493	With Christ in the School of Prayer
9789390575602	Your Faith is Your Fortune
9789390575473	Your Infinite Power To Be Rich
9789390575251	Your Word is Your Wand
9789390575718	Youth
9789391316099	A Christmas Carol
9789391316105	A Doll's House
9789391316501	A Passage to India
9789391316709	A Portrait of the Artist as a Young Man
9789391316112	A Tale of Two Cities
9789391316747	A Tear and a Smile
9789391316167	Agnes Gray
9789391316174	Alice's Adventures in Wonderland
9789391316136	Anandamath
9789391316181	Anne Of Green Gables
9789391316754	Anthem
9789391316198	Around The World in 80 Days
9789391316013	As A Man Thinketh
9789391316242	Autobiography of a Yogi
9789391316266	Beyond Good and Evil
9789391316761	Bleak House
9789391316778	Chitra, a Play in One Act
9789391316310	David Copperfield

9789391316075	Demian
9789391316785	Dubliners
9789391316051	Favourite Tales from the Arabian Nights
9789391316235	Gitanjali
9789391316068	Gravity
9789391316150	Great Speeches of Abraham Lincoln
9789391316662	Guerilla Warfare
9789391316839	Kim
9789391316822	Mother
9789391316211	My Childhood
9789391316846	Nationalism
9789391316327	Oliver Twist
9789391316853	Pygmalion
9789391316334	Relativity: The Special and the General Theory
9789391316389	Scientific Healing Affirmation
9789391316341	Sons and Lovers
9789391316587	Tales from India
9789391316372	Tess of The D'Urbervilles
9789391316396	The Awakening and Selected Stories
9789391316402	The Bhagvad Gita
9789391316303	The Book of Enoch
9789391316228	The Canterville Ghost
9789391316907	The Dynamic Laws of Prosperity
9789391316006	The Great Gatsby
9789391316860	The Hungry Stones and Other Stories
9789391316433	The Idiot
9789391316440	The Importance of Being Earnest
9789391316297	The Light of Asia
9789391316914	The Madman His Parables and Poems
9789391316457	The Odyssey
9789391316921	The Picture of Dorian Gray
9789391316464	The Prince
9789391316938	The Prophet
9789391316945	The Republic
9789391316518	The Scarlet Letter

9789391316143	The Seven Laws of Teaching
9789391316525	The Story of My Experiments with Truth
9789391316532	The Tales of the Mother Goose
9789391316549	The Thirty Nine Steps
9789391316594	The Time Machine
9789391316600	The Turn of the Screw
9789391316983	The Upanishads
9789391316617	The Yellow Wallpaper
9789391316426	The Yoga Sutras of Patanjali
9789391316990	Ulysses
9789391316624	Utopia
9789391316679	Vanity Fair
9789391316020	What Is To Be Done
9789391316686	Within A Budding Grove
9789391316693	Women in Love